PARENTS:
ADOLESCENTS ARE
ADULTS-WITH-LESS-SENSE

PARENTS:
ADOLESCENTS ARE
ADULTS-WITH-LESS-SENSE

*A Christ-Centered Approach
to Adolescent Development*

Winston B. Stanley, PhD

iUniverse, Inc.
Bloomington

Parents: Adolescents Are Adults-with-Less-Sense
A Christ-Centered Approach to Adolescent Development

iUniverse books may be ordered through booksellers or by contacting:

iUniverse
1663 Liberty Drive
Bloomington, IN 47403
www.iuniverse.com
1-800-Authors (1-800-288-4677)

ISBN: 978-1-4759-6496-7 (sc)
ISBN: 978-1-4759-6498-1 (hc)
ISBN: 978-1-4759-6497-4 (ebk)

Library of Congress Control Number: 2012922730

Printed in the United States of America

iUniverse rev. date: 1/18/2013

Bible verses in this book were as written in King James Version (KJV) unless otherwise noted. Other Bibles noted are New International Version (NIV) and New King James Version (NKJV). Clear Word Paraphrase

Higher than the highest human thoughts can reach is God's ideal for His Children.

Ellen G. White

Our greatest natural resource is the minds of our children.

Walter Elias Disney

Dedicated to my only son, Courtney Michael Stanley,
and
Applegate Adventist Junior Academy

CONTENTS

FOREWORD

There is an old saying: "the apple doesn't fall too far from the tree." This principle is true on both divine and human planes. Christ was the spitting image of His Father, and children are the spitting image of their parents. I found this to be best illustrated by Monica and Anna, who are daughters of Art and Cindy Villarreal, a Christian family I know. Monica has physical features resembling their father but personality traits of their mother. Anna, on the other hand, has physical features resembling their mother, with personality traits resembling their father. I have often joked with my wife about their uniqueness, how God tweaked the Villarreals' DNA while displaying a type of Divine humor. Granted, we are all born sinners with similar inherited and cultivated propensities to evil. When judged properly and placed under the biblical microscope, there should be an increased level of tolerance and patience on behalf of parents and less rebellion coming from the adolescent in light of the love, patience, and tolerance God has shown us. This explains the purpose for which this book is written. With this in mind, I write this book.

PREFACE

The chapters of this book are a condensed expression of my many years of pastoring, counseling, and attending youth conferences, camporees, and retreats, along with my many enjoyable experiences and activities spent with developing adolescents. From the heart, this book is my personal, loving tribute. This is my way of defending the developing adolescent and a unique way of sharing wisdom, experiences, and research with the public. I have compiled all of these things in one source that I think can help steer parents, adolescents, and those who work with youth in a positive direction. Needless to say, not only did my youthful friends keep me on my aging toes, but each left a little of themselves—framed, hanging as a portrait on the walls of my memory. Most of those memories were joyful, although some were painful. However, the imprints are all collected there, etched in time.

INTRODUCTION

As a pastor and youth counselor, I have discovered that every concerned parent wants a balanced child. Balance really involves four basic components: the mental, the physical, the spiritual, and the social. With that said, the Bible speaks of Christ's adolescence as very balanced. Luke 2:52 states, "And Jesus increased in wisdom [mental] and stature [physical], and in favour with God [spiritual] and man [social]," making Christ our supreme mentor and example. Furthermore, as a parent, I am more thankful the biblical record substantiates that Christ was "in all points [adolescence and all] tempted like us" so that He could understand our nature and struggles firsthand.

Parents, adolescents are simply "adults-with-less-sense" with inherited, and sometimes cultivated, at-risk behaviors. Many make the common mistake that this relatively short period, comparatively speaking, is a time described as the period of life known as the "less years"—a directionless, emotionless, fearless period—or a time in the growth processes when it is difficult to know what is going on in a teen's mind. Many have defined adolescence as the rebellion period in the life of the developing young adult. However, we may want to label or define adolescence; adolescence is actually a transitional period, lasting from ten to twelve years, in the life of the developing youth that can involve all of the above.

When toying with the idea of writing on adolescence or the adolescent mind, I did not have to go very far for research, because my one and only child is currently evolving through that late adolescent period. More intrusively, I peered deep into my own soul, recalling those adolescent years or that period of young adult evolution. Actually, adolescence does not have to be a period of rebellion as much as a transformation into young adulthood.

Outside my study window, I have my version of a rose garden—pristine yellow, rosy red, girly pink, and velvet white roses ranging in all distinct colors and sizes. The beauty of it all is to watch their transformation into full bloom under God's morning sun sprinkled by a light morning shower. What beauty to behold as I watch roses develop from a short distance in a relatively short period of time. This period of adolescence can be the same—a beautiful transformation into young adulthood viewed and watched from a short distance in a short period of time.

With the Bible as the adolescent's guidebook, I recommend that adolescents spend fifteen minutes of devotional time daily in contemplation of the life of Christ, reading from the Gospels[1] in meditation and prayer. This devotional time will help spur balance and spiritual growth for the adolescent. Not only will a devotional life assist in balance and growth, but it will make this rite of passage into young adulthood much easier and happier for the adolescent and the parents.

I write this book with two objectives in mind. The first objective is to cover the transitional period of adolescence from a biblical perspective. The second is to assist the parents, adolescents, and lay leaders to see the importance of setting a proper foundation that will affect the adolescents' decision-making process the rest of their lives. Parents, adolescents, and lay leaders, as you read this book, keep in mind that adolescents are nothing more but young adults-with-less-sense.

---

[1]   Matthew, Mark, Luke, and John.

PART I

UNDERSTANDING THE ADOLESCENT

CHAPTER ONE

STAGES OF ADOLESCENT DEVELOPMENT

God's Ideal: A Thinking Adolescent

I happened to run upon this statement doing research in education: "The mind that depends upon the judgments of others is certain, sooner or later, to be mis-led."[2] In essence, the writer is saying we must learn early on to think for our individual selves. Years ago, my college professor stated, "the objective of a book is to make you think." Over the years, I have come to discover that both statements are true. With this said, the most recent research by neuroscientists involves what's called the field of functional magnetic resonance imaging, or fMRI. This technique allows researchers to monitor the blood flow through parts of the brain as it responds to both external and internal stimuli, enabling researchers to monitor which parts of the brain are active and which are resting. Though the technique is being eagerly explored in a variety of fields, fMRI has received criticism from some brain experts as being the modern-day equivalent of phrenology.[3] The question is, what can it tell researchers about the inner workings of the human brain and, more so, the adolescent brain?

As far back as I can remember, there has always been this insatiable desire by scientists to peer into the inner workings of the human brain. I'm sure there have been times as a parent when you have asked yourself, "Where was his mind when he did that?" The very same question can be asked of Adam and Eve: "What on Earth were they thinking when they made that ginormous mistake?" A great feat of science—or maybe

---

[2]   E. G. White, *Education*, 231.
[3]   Phrenology is the idea that the sizes of brain areas were meaningful and could be inferred by examining the skull of an individual.

not—would be to create an instrument where we could peer into the adolescent's mind in an attempt to figure out what actually makes them tick. Or try to figure out what's going in their heads. After five minutes of looking at their brain circuitry—a bunch of disconnected wires—and active blood flow of external stimuli, we would probably shut down or abandon the experiment for lack of understanding. The fMRI may reveal active blood flow, but it will fall far short of disclosing active theoretical reasoning.

In the article by Molly Edmonds titled, "Are Teen Brains Really Different from Adult Brains," she says, "The teenage brain doesn't appear to work like this—the Adults Brain. For comparison's sake, think of the teenage brain as an entertainment center that hasn't been fully hooked up. There are loose wires, so that the speaker system isn't working with the DVD player, which in turn hasn't been formatted to work with the television yet. And to top it all off, the remote control hasn't even arrived!"[4] This book is an attempt to give you somewhat of an idea of the wiring process and to assist the adolescent toward making the right connections that would help them arrive safely on adulthood shores.

However, the following question needs to be asked: what is God's ideal for the developing adolescent? I vividly remember my eighth grade teacher Ms. Holden challenging us to "tink, young people, tink [think]!" She never could get that emphatic *h* correct, but she certainly got her point across with relative ease. While it was also pounded into our heads by many to "be a leader and not a follower," Ms. Holden challenged us to be thinkers.

From the very beginning, God would have the developing adolescent utilize her thinking capabilities. At creation, the antediluvians—men and women before the flood—were considered giants, standing some sixteen to eighteen feet tall with man's female counterpart standing head and shoulder next to him. Their intellectual capacity equaled their physical size in giant proportion. There are human marvels to this day that baffle the modern mind—for example, the pyramids of ancient Egypt and the sundial with its precision timing, just to mention a couple—that reflect their thinking creative abilities. These creations cause one to be impressed by yesteryear's thinking humanity.

---

4   Molly Edmonds, Howstuffworks.com.

In Deuteronomy 3:1–11, we read of a giant people whose houses were constructed of huge black stones in order to make their buildings absolutely impregnable to any force that could have been brought against them. The inhabitants of this land—descendants from a giant race—were themselves of tremendous size and strength, yet they became distinguished for their violence and cruelty as to be the terror of all surrounding nations. Og, the king of the country, was remarkable for his size and prowess, even in a nation of giants.[5] Unfortunately, with this people, their intellects were used in a most negative and destructive manner.

However, it all began at creation when the intelligence and creativity of God was clearly orchestrated from the invention of the first delicately tinted flower to the superior craftsmanship of both male and female, from the naming of the animal kingdom to the ascribing of the first given name Eve, the mother of all creation. Man was created in the image of God with great thinking capacity. I am grateful that every created human being was created in God's image and endowed with powers akin to that of the Creator—with individuality and power to think and do. Because we are created in the image of God, this means that we can take responsibility for our own actions and that we are not slaves of circumstances but instead liberated human beings.

It has been substantiated that during the transitional years, adolescents are learning to think critically, and freedom of expression becomes increasingly important as they are learning to act or contract as an adult. The learned set of values (ethical, moral, and religious), as taught by parents and institutions during these adolescent years, will be challenged and questioned by the developing adolescent mind, which makes the establishment of rules significantly important for homes and institutions. While education is important during these years, adolescents seek answers to real issues in life, which make them question their learned system of values.

While there is still the need for discipline, rules, and restrictions for the adolescent, parents and institutions should be careful *not* to restrict or hamper the adolescent's freedom of expression in the religious and social arena. Instead, they should be careful to offer guidance and support and encourage a principled, critical-thinking adolescent. Author and writer

---

[5]   White, *Patriarchs and Prophets*, 435.

E. G. White profoundly states, "youth are to be thinkers and not reflectors of other men's thoughts."[6]

Psychologist Judith Nembhard[7] writes, "a good thinker learns to analyze ideas, separating facts from fallacies." In the progressive educational years from grade school to college, we can see this process at work. In the Christian arena, critical thinking involves examining issues and ideas in order to make sound judgments based on facts rather than personal opinions or unsubstantiated biblical doctrinal beliefs. Research has proven, according to Nembhard, that the ability to think critically can be improved with practice. Christians, who must always be interested in knowing the truth and discriminating between truth and error, ought to be keenly interested in developing their critical-thinking skills. This is also true for the developing adolescent. However, in order for the adolescent to do this, he or she must have knowledge and, in this case, factual biblical knowledge.

I have often sat in religious meetings where leaders encourage youth to follow Christianity. But until a biblical precedence is established based on biblical fact, a thinking adolescent will always challenge the established system of beliefs. There must be supporting facts in order to draw accurate conclusions relative to religious systems in their upbringing. Not only that, but when adolescents question or challenge an established systems of beliefs, they are seeking practical tools or principles for constructive living. During these adolescent years, teens are looking for substantiated facts based on a practical biblical context.

Keavin Hayden,[8] commenting on the Christian lifestyle relative to adolescents, believes parents of developing adolescent Christians need to move outside of their comfort zones to accommodate some of the desires of their developing children. Granted, leaving this parental comfort zone does not mean violating principle. Hayden believes that even though parents may not always agree with their children's desires and ideas, as they grow and develop as adolescents and as the parents get older, the parents must play the role of a wise counselor, allowing their children to make their own choices. Hayden believes forceful, manipulative, overbearing attitudes or legalistic rules relative to certain Christian standards will

---

6   White, *Education*, 20.

7   Nembhard, *A Critical Thinker? Or Merely Critical?*, 20.

8   Hayden, *Lifestyle of the Remnant*, 127.

never succeed in wedding a youthful heart to Christ, which is the ultimate challenge. "Violating another's free-will only mis-represent God." Our job as the wise counselors is to get the adolescent to *think principally*. Hayden believes there is a fine balance in Christianity between that which is real and that which is ideal.[9]

If I can paraphrase one writer, substantiated by personal research, "adolescents seek an environment where they do not have to park their brains." This is of supreme importance with adolescents entering the college years. They want to be able—even encouraged—to think for themselves and play an active role in implementing programs rather than having everything laid out for them. They desire dialogue. Roger Dudley, a denominational youth counselor, states, "while we as a church have had a good deal of focus on children and youth, investing in them our best resources, there is evidence to suggest that they are not encouraged (generally speaking) to evaluate critically their faith, to question it, to re-think it for themselves or to personally redefine it."[10] Our challenge as parents, leaders, pastors, etc. is to encourage principled, critical-thinking adolescents. As Ms. Holden so often encouraged, "Tink, young people, tink!"

Adolescence Defined: What Exactly Is It?

The historical Western view of adolescence has tended to lean more toward defining adolescence in a vacuum period called the "teen years" from ages thirteen to nineteen. However, adolescence, when viewed from scripture and more progressive learning—depending on the individual—can start early or late with some and may extend well beyond the age of nineteen, depending on the individual and circumstances. Scripture defines adolescence as moving from childhood to manhood.[11] From a research perspective, I would tend to describe adolescence as the stage of development between childhood and adulthood rather than from a confining period (ages thirteen to nineteen). Some often refer to adolescence as a transitional period in the life of an individual. Tripp

---

9   Ibid.

10   Dudley, *Why Teenagers leave the Church*, 197.

11   1 Corinthians 13:11.

defines the adolescent years as years of change, insecurity, and tumult.[12] Bancroft and Reinisch describes the stages of adolescence as early (ages twelve to fourteen), middle (ages fifteen to seventeen), and late (ages eighteen to twenty-three).[13]

Historically, the term *adolescence* was used by Greeks to refer to physical growth and not necessarily mental maturity. You can be an adolescent in body and not fully in mind. In our Western society, adulthood was assigned to all those who passed grammar school. If you reached eleven or twelve, you were considered an adult. If you did not continue on to grammar school, chores were assigned to the individual to perform the role of an adult. Adolescence was defined more by what you did rather than your level of mental, emotional, or social maturity.

There were basically three reasons for maturity in the middle and late eighteenth and nineteenth centuries. First, there was the early death of parents. Circumstantially, in the 1860s, people died younger due to lack of advanced medical and physiological knowledge, resulting in children being forced into adulthood early and taking on adultlike responsibilities. Second, agrarian lifestyle required teens to live as adults, performing the duties of adults in order to sustain. Families were sizable, and chores and duties were assigned according to gender. In the current generation, adolescence goes back to the industrial revolution. In the rural areas, children developed faster. They worked the farm, awaking early to milk the cows, feed the chickens, etc. More was expected of them, which tremendously accelerated their maturity level.

A third reason for maturation was that families did not garner enough income to sustain and support themselves. Once a child developed financially self-supporting capabilities, they moved away from home. Today, in Western society, maturity can now be correlated with or commences when the adolescent leaves home for college, whereas with rural adolescent the majority of education and training was the responsibility of the family. Today, the education and training for an occupation is done by society or culture. Adolescents living in rural areas grew and developed faster because more was required of them. We must

---

12   Kangas, J., "A study of the religious attitudes and behaviors of Seventh-day Adventist adolescents in North America related to their family, educational, and church backgrounds," (Ed. Dissertation, Andrews University, 1988), 45
13   Ibid., 45.

keep in mind that while maturation depends a lot on the individual child, circumstances and experiences can certainly speed up the process, which explains why some adults and adolescents are considered more mature than others. Today, urban or city teens, on the whole, tend to develop slower because they have fewer duties and less responsibility is required of them. In urban areas during the industrial age, adolescents tended to have an apprenticeship or were trained for certain occupations. Today, as compared to the past, developing adolescents attend college to be educated for various occupations.

Biological or medical adolescence begins with the body bombardment of hormonal changes that result in a growth surge and reproduction maturation and ends when growth peaks near twenty-one to twenty-three years of age.[14] According to David Pruit, the author of *Your Adolescent*, for some adolescents, this onslaught of changes is tantamount to being on an emotional roller coaster, which is a difficult ride for the developing teen and his family. Hersch[15] sums up the period of adolescence as "increasingly the period in a teens life with its own values, ethics, rules, worldview, rites of passage, worries, joys, and momentum." Bancroft and Reinisch believe adolescence is a transitional period of development that varies from culture to culture and is a time when individuals learn to be socially responsible for themselves and for their actions.[16]

Brain Circuitry: The Psychological Mind of the Adolescent

My dad would often say, "Son, use your head for more than a hat rack." Again, I think we can conclude one thing: the brain circuitry of the adolescent is most interesting to observe to say the least. As stated earlier, adolescent development can be divided into three stages: early, middle, and late. The precise age for this change may be difficult to define, but you can definitely calculate that it will be around a certain time when changes start to occur. It is during these developmental stages that most guidance,

---

[14] Hines, *Counseling Troubled Youth* (taped notes), Trinity Seminary. Newburgh, Ind., 2003.

[15] Hersch, Patricia, *A Tribe Apart: A Journey into the Heart of American Adolescence* (New York: Fawcett Columbine, 1998), 12.

[16] Kanjas, J. 75

direction, and advice are needed. It is a time when the adolescent is filled with doubts and uncertainties. However, at the same time during this period, important decisions are being made for the future. The Christian parents' duty is twofold: to teach their children to live successfully in today's culture, while at the same time preparing them for the Kingdom of God. See graphic below:

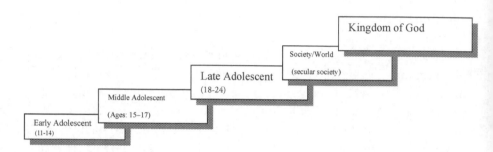

According to Focus Adolescent Services, the adolescent period of the teens life is not so simple for the individual. While adults carry on the very same tasks of growth and development themselves and have a greater sense of who they are, what they value, what they need, and how best to get what they need, teenagers are in the process of learning, making mistakes, using poor judgment, or being impulsive. These are all parts of this developmental process. Counterculture looks—a pierced eyebrow, green or purple stripes in the hair, or pierced body parts—can be annoying to parents and adults; however, they are also a move toward autonomy and a statement of identity.

While adults encounter these same challenges, they are usually better prepared to meet the challenges than adolescents. As adolescents develop, their major task is to become their own people. Focus Adolescent Services further observed that adolescents are to learn to make choices and commitments, follow through with them, and stand up independently in the world.[17]

The adolescent has a rather delicate individual psychology. Brain maturation, coupled with everyday experiences, result in a new wiring process that enhances thinking capabilities. As the adolescent grows older, his thinking becomes more abstract and fused with the practical.

---

[17]   http://wwwFocusas.com, *Help Your Teen* Focus 2000, (accessed 12 Sept. 2008).

During this period, teens swing back and forth between dependence and independence as they work on these tasks. It is easy for parents to become frustrated with their developing teens while this transition is happening. It is also easy during this period for a parent to assume that if the adolescent would simply follow the plan that makes sense, things would be all right in the end. However, you will come to find that adolescents often deviate from the defined plan, which makes life frustrating for both parent and adolescent.

During this time, the adolescent is an explorer, discovering himself. Self-esteem in girls seems to be more fragile during these years because of the emphasis on physical attractiveness. Some say this decline in self-esteem is only temporary; however, there are times that certain issues need to be dealt with during these adolescent years. If they aren't, teens can suffer for the rest of their lives because of unresolved issues. Most adolescents, it is believed, eventually reclaim their self-esteem. We must keep in mind when dealing with the developing mind that there are exceptions to the rule.

As the adolescent's reasoning abilities increase, he begins to focus more on the deeper questions of right and wrong: What kind of person do I want to be? How do I react in certain situations? When is it important to stand firm, and when is there room to be flexible? Adolescence can be a period in life when there is serious introspection going on. Some would label this period a time of selfishness for the developing adolescent.

During middle school years, the adolescent's moral development continues to evolve as he becomes more aware of relationships between the individual and society. At this stage, a teen is more likely to conform to the views of society—he will accept the notion that laws are there for a purpose and that those who break them must pay a price. As the adolescent gets older, the adolescents thinking shifts to a new plane. He is able to view moral conflicts in more abstract terms; he realizes that widespread societal views do not always reflect the moral high ground. He may decide that certain moral behavior has to be above that of the law or societal norm. He is developing the moral standards by which the rest of his life will be lived. During this time, parents can observe the impact of society on child. There is a new circuitry going on. Here is the time when modeling and mentoring is important in the life of the developing the child.

Forming an identity is also important during this time. Erik Erikson theorized that a person must work through four development issues on the way to forming an identity during adolescence: trust (process by which a teen seeks and finds friends who are trustworthy and admirable), autonomy (the teen begins to chart an independent course instead of simply going along with parental wishes), initiative (the teen sets her own goals), and industry (the older adolescent realization as she progresses through adolescence that she alone must take responsibility for setting goals and for the quality of work she does toward achieving those goals).[18]

While the adolescent is experiencing these psychological changes, according to adolescent psychologist, Beth Livermore, "during this time we are laying down the basic circuitry of the brain. As we grow up, the world subsequently makes its mark physically. Exposure to novel tasks and novel stimuli generates the development of new circuits and synapses for handling all of them. From then on, continued stimulation throughout life further strengthens these pathways and enhances their interconnections."[19]

According to Livermore, scientists cannot yet quantify exactly how much an enriched environment helps the brains of young children to grow. But "we do know that deprivation and isolation can result in failure of the brain to form its rich set of connections,"[20] says Don Shatz. Livermore further believes:

> whether it's a new sensation or a fresh idea, every outside stimulus is first converted into electrical signals as it enters the cranium. These electrical signals trundle down known pathways, splitting off into multiple directions for processing. Where the lack of prior experience has left no established route, the signal will forge a new one, linking neuron to neuron as it travels along. The resulting chain is called a brain circuit, and the next time the same stimulus enters the brain, it speeds efficiently along its old route, now grooved into an expressway. Hundreds of millions of brain circuits are created by millions of experiences. Sometime near the high-school prom age—around 18 years old—networks stop forming. We are hard-wired by the end of adolescence. Each of us is left with a "brain-print," or network

---

[18] E. H. Erikson, *Identity: Youth and Crisis*, 35.
[19] Livermore, *Build a Better Brain*, 128.
[20] Ibid., 75.

system, which like a fingerprint, is unique to each one of us. This is the hardware that processes our thoughts.[21]

Sexual Development: The Tender Box of Hormones

One of the most explosive topics to be discussed when dealing with the adolescent is sex. As a matter of fact, we tend to take a type of laissez-faire, hands-off approach to the topic. Actually, adolescents enjoy discussing this topic, unlike their parents who subject themselves to Victorian and religious restraints. Oh, how they enjoy dabbling into the "untouchable" to discuss—unknown to them—the raging hormones of puberty. That wonderful tenderbox of hormones created by God somehow triggers a type of electrochemical charge that stimulates the developing reproductive organs.

I have often wondered how it all starts. Does it start with the lower abdominal reproductive organs triggering the brain? Or does it begin in the brain, which then proceeds to trigger reproductive organs? If I suggest it starts with the lower anatomical regions (the reproductive organs), then I am suggesting it is body or "matter over mind." If I suggest it starts in the brain, then I contend it's "mind over matter." I would prefer to accept the latter—mind over matter, where I can say I have the moral upper hand and decision making is key. These are unanswered questions that continue to puzzle us. However, what we can conclude physiologically is that one impacts the other, and they both work as a harmonious whole.

When you think about the developing process of the human anatomy, one can rationally conclude that we are incredibly and wonderfully made creatures of God. The complexity of our physical bodies remains one of the most powerful testimonies to the wisdom and might of our Creator. To capture the reproductive process by cinematic slow motion would indeed be a thrill to watch. Or perhaps even more thrilling would be to enroll in the class of Anatomy and Physiology 101 where we could sit under the tutelage of God as He explains how He chose to create male and female before proceeding into a divine laboratory where we could watch the thrills of the creation of humanity piece by piece unfold before us. What a feat that would be! Maybe God will take us into His personal

---

[21] Ibid., 50.

science lab to give us a firsthand, detailed look into how He designed man and woman and what He originally intended for us as creation's best. Until then, we can only conclude that we are incredible and wonderful creatures made by our Creator.

When we mention change with reference to the adolescent, puberty becomes a big part of the change, but not the whole change as society would have us conclude. The changes that occur within we cannot see, but external changes definitely can be seen through physical development. Sigmund Freud, the renowned secular psychologist, traces most of man's problems back to sexuality. However, the Christian counselor and psychologist traces man's problems back to his fall in sin.

With this said, it would be best for the developing adolescent to give study to the study of sexuality with parental support through discussion within a Christian setting and environment. I shall never forget when this topic was introduced at our Church youth meeting. I thought it best to present this topic in a nonthreatening, educational, Christian setting. Even with careful scrutiny and set parameters, this topic went forth with a supercharged discussion. In order to lighten the existing tension of the topic, I borrowed carefully selected material regarding sexual reproduction from the local community library for educational purposes. I decided to introduce the topic of sex by using an animated video of parents joyously engaging in the act of sex while covered by bed sheets in a vibrating bed and surrounded by floating hearts. Needless to say, this was a very bold experiment. However, it helps tremendously to know one's audience and have them be familiar with the facilitator.

From a Christian perspective, the video had been made in good taste. Parents were seated in the rear, cringing with shamefacedness, while their developing adolescents were on edge, bursting with laughter. At the same time, the youth leaders and I were, in essence, having fun watching it all play out with sophisticated, restrained humor. Frankly, it was an unforgettable viewing. The video was literally filled with profound educational points for the adolescent. One parent edged forward and whispered in my ear, "Pastor, make sure you clarify this part of the video with your personal, edited comments." I kept a straight face, but deep inside, I was on the edge of my seat in total laughter. What's my point? Because of the sensitive nature of the topic, encourage leaders and parents to move with sound biblical caution, but by all means, do move ahead with positive Christian discussion.

Parents, teens, and leaders are to keep in mind that sexual emotions start in the brain circuitry system; what begins in the mind can also be controlled by the mind—a type of mind over matter. Once this is understood, it needs to be clearly stated that sex should be viewed from a biblical context, with wires connected to God. Society has already prepared an answer that sex is an act carried out by two consenting adults, which opens the door for a philosophy of guilt-free sex without biblical parameters. Further physiological research substantiates that this change in the life of the adolescent, if not kept in check, can lead to mood swings and phenomenal stress.

As a pastor, I do believe adolescents need to be aware of occurring changes taking place in their bodies, not just from a physiological perspective but also because of external pressures placed on them by society. The complexity of our physical bodies remains one of the most powerful testimonies to the wisdom and might of our Creator. When viewed from its proper biblical perspective, puberty can be understood best by the defined roles given adolescents by God, from that very first nocturnal emission[22] (wet dream) for males and the lubrication of the vaginal area for the female.

Both male and female adolescent must understand that these emissions produced by the male organs are the body's natural means of dispelling semen in a premarital state. Any other artificial methods prescribed for this natural process are highly discouraged. However, nocturnal emissions may happen any time during or after puberty. For both male and female, the so-called wet dream or emission is a wonderful experience. It is a way for the body to tell the developing adolescent, "There is something wonderful going on deep inside." It's as if the body is shouting, "Watch out! You now possess the physiological tools physically to reproduce life that is biblically prescribed to be enjoyed with the marriage parameters."

On the other hand, for the female, menstruation (or period) shouts to the young developing female, "You are now at the reproductive age to sustain and reproduce life." Factors such as heredity, diet (which we will discuss later), and overall health can accelerate or decelerate the menstruation process. Sexual development really starts prior to adolescence, much earlier in the life of the child. However, during this transitional period,

---

22   Nocturnal emissions are so named because the majority of occurrences happen while sleeping.

sex takes on a totally new perspective. Physiologically, when the preceding takes place, the adolescent has now entered into Life's Course Sex 101.

Much discussion and deliberation has been given to the topic of sex education in schools. Having grown up with parents who were Victorian in thinking, I would not have known the scientific aspect of sex education had it not been taught during PE in middle school. It so happened that during that same time I experienced my first wet dream, Coach Porter was instructing us on the basics of the sexual reproductive organs. This raises another question: should sex education be taught in public and private schools? My response—why not! Roland Martin, the CNN syndicated columnist and author, states it best:

> How in the world do we say it's okay for schools to teach our children about math, science, history, and numerous other subjects, yet then get high and mighty with righteous indignation when biology is taken a step further to focus on sex? Too many parents live in denial about their children having sex, and somehow saying you'll handle the tough stuff is living in fantasy land. … Abstinence is definitely the safest of all safe sex measures, but there is also a point when we have to accept reality. Talk to school teachers and administrators and they will tell you that students as young as middle school are engaging in oral sex, and there is the belief that that really doesn't count as sex. Yet anyone with half a brain knows that to be the case. If kids are out there having oral sex, they sure as heck need to know that doing so without protection can be life-altering. But such parents groups prefer to stick their heads in the sand. They find such talk unseemly and think such frankness should be left between child and parent. Not me.

> As a Jesus lovin' Christian, I'm about real talk, and if that means dealing with sex directly, let's go for it. … Right-thinking folks are tired of seeing young folks coming back HIV-positive or dealing with a pregnancy at 16. I have nine nieces and four nephews, and I would be fully supportive of them being taught about sex education in school. Forget shying from a tough subject. If we are going to equip our children for tomorrow, then sex needs to be dealt with in a smart, productive, and

educational setting by professionals. It's clear that parents aren't as dependable on some matters as they like to delude themselves into believing.[23]

While I am in full agreement with Roland Martin, might I also suggest during adolescence that sexual activity is in full throttle emotionally. Most pastors would suggest to the parent that "it's praying time now." The brain's emotional center—the limbic system—is "a tinderbox of emotions," according to neurologist Dr. Ronald Dahl.[24] Hormones have now become an important part of the teen's brain circuitry system. To try and explain the change scientifically can become confusing. The only thing that can be said is that we are creatively and wonderfully made. If this part of life can be guarded and kept in check, the marriage institution can be one of utter fulfillment.

Physical Development

In Western culture, adolescence can cover a span of almost ten to twelve years, from puberty to full biological maturation. Within this time frame, youths are affected by various developmental transformations. Physically, the average boy begins his growth spurt around twelve. For girls, the average growth spurt starts around ten. During this early adolescent period the boy may grow as much as nine inches to his height. Most girls add six inches to their height. Different parts of the body grow at different rates. Typically, the legs grow faster than the trunk or any other part of the body.

Educational Development

Educationally, the American culture views the years of middle school, high school, and college as the period of adolescence. Psychologically, adolescence ends when the teen has the ability to contract (make decisions) as an adult and is able to sustain himself apart from his parents.

---

[23]   CNN (Cable News Network) contributor.
[24]   Ronald Dahl, Psychologist at the University of Pittsburgh, PA.

It is also believed that the main task of adolescence is for teenagers to learn—a type of learning where you are not just getting the right answer but seeking applied knowledge for personal development.[25] Most importantly during this transitional phase is for the adolescent to understand the meaning behind the right answer. The "right answer" is something that adolescents responsibly build up to, gained from lessons of experience. This is the difficult work of the adolescent, and it requires support from parents, relatives, church members, and neighbors.

Spiritual Development

Many people experience religious conversion during their adolescent years. Reflecting back on my adolescent development, my relationship with Christ certainly helped guide me through turbulence during that time, if there was a period of turbulence. Faith development is critical during this period. Biblical maturity is a must for the adolescent. Here is where church action programs and community action youth groups can be of tremendous service. Because adolescence is a period of growth and change physically, educationally, and psychologically, full physical maturity is not reached until the body stops physical growth in the early to midtwenties. It can be safely concluded that the adolescent's mind—which is a part of culture—is in motion or operating almost *twice* as fast as the mind of a fully developed adult-based on external and internal physiological development. Consider first that the adolescent's mind is experiencing natural internal growth with the development of brain circuitry, as stated by adolescent psychologist Beth Livermore.[26] Second, the internal growth is combined with the bombardment of external stimuli by culture, which enters the brain through the "avenues of the soul" (sight, taste, touch, hearing, smell) and creates heightened activity. When sleeping or resting, it is also confirmed that the brain continues to be actively engaged through dreams, even in adulthood.

Dr. Jay Geidd has studied the development of the adolescent/teen brain; he describes massive development of brain infrastructure during the adolescent teen years. The frontal lobe, which is concerned with

---

[25] http://wwwFocusas.com, *Help Your Teen 2000, (accessed 12 Sept. 2008)*.
[26] Beth Livermore, *Build a Better Brain*, 48.

prioritizing, thinking ahead, and planning, is just developing. Areas dealing with "gut responses" are overly active. The cerebellum, according to Geidd, which functions as the instrument of abstract learning and motor skills, is developing. Thus, the physical brain is changing and impacting the adolescent's perceptions. The picture that emerges is of a crucial developmental period during which enormous changes are occurring inside, and great care needs to be exerted by those in caring and guiding roles. Adolescents need security and positive communication to help them reinterpret emotional and situational information.[27]

Dr. Geidd points out the tragedy that just as the brain is carrying out this new development, many adolescents are experimenting with drugs and chemicals that can alter their brain functioning and development. At such a sensitive point in growth, one choice can affect how the brain will function for the rest of someone's life. Therefore, because of the ever-changing status of the adolescent during this period, biblical maturity[28] or a meaningful relationship with Christ can be a vital asset.[29]

During this time, adolescents develop their ideology and theology.[30] It can be concluded that some adolescents become very focused on finding a person or system that replaces the parents as role models. This replacement process can be called *transference*. Adolescents are seemingly searching for things that enhance their independence from their parents and allow them to be responsible for their own behavior. Sydney Lewis states:

> In our culture, adolescence is a period during which a young person undergoes physical, emotional, intellectual, social, and spiritual growth. While who they are reveals itself slowly, and often in deep, intangible ways, they are actively, moment by moment, establishing who they are not by testing the tethers which bind them to parents, teachers, and peers. It requires great energy to undertake the passage from family to worldly

---

[27]   Geidd, J. *Interviews with Jay Geid.* 130

[28]   Biblical maturity is that point in the adolescent's life when he recognizes he is a sinner and spiritual regeneration is needed.

[29]   Ibid 75

[30]   V. Gillespie, E. Boyatt, and B. Gane, *Valuegenesis: Ten Years Later,* 72.

life; and great understanding, attention, and concern on the part of parents who must come to know their children anew.[31]

In conclusion, G. Stanley Hall, the first president of the American Psychological Association (APA), argued that adolescence is indeed a time of great turbulence and tumult.[32] During this time, parents need a tremendous amount of godly patience. Psychoanalytical work, like that of Sigmund Freud, also argues that adolescence is a period of time in the life of the youth that is inevitably fraught with parent-child conflict. While adolescence can be labeled a period of physical, psychological, educational, and spiritual metamorphosis, this process is not always displayed in the Eriksonian expression "negative identity,"[33] which is another term for rebellion. Margaret Mead, the great anthropologist, on the other hand, in *Coming of Age in Samoa*, argued that the adolescent years, given the appropriate cultural context, could be years of gradual, *peaceful* transition to young adulthood rather than a period of rebellion.[34] Rebellion during the adolescent years is simply an acting out of negative behaviors triggered by the child's intrinsic sinful nature. This behavior can be corrected with guidance from the three most influential institutions in the adolescent's life: the home, the church, and the school. These three institutions will be discussed at length later.

Taking Responsibility

One area that needs to be emphasized with the adolescent is the need to take responsibility. The term *responsibility* is considered to be the elephant sitting in the room from which the child or developing adolescent cannot escape. As stated earlier, it is believed that legally the period of adolescence ends when the youth has achieved the ability to contract as an adult. I used the term *contract* in the sense that the adolescent is able to negotiate and make mature decisions in life independent of her parents. Thus, the adolescent will never outgrow wise counsel, which she will need at

---

[31] Lewis, *A Totally Alien Life*, 17.
[32] Benjamin, L. T. *Stanley Hall Lecture Series.* vol. 1, pp. 1
[33] Ibid., 181.
[34] Margaret Mead, *Coming of Age in Samoa*, 50.

certain junctures in life, but with that counsel, she will draw her own conclusions.

We should keep in mind that part of the parents' job is to assist the developing adolescent in getting to that place of responsibility. When the adolescent is able to say, "I take responsibility," know with certainty that he has reached a certain milestone and that a great task has been accomplished.

CHAPTER TWO

BIBLICAL CONCEPT OF ADOLESCENCE
(Adolescence as Defined in Scripture)

Little is recorded in scripture during the adolescent years of Jesus. The Gospel writer Luke appears to be the most comprehensive and detailed of all. Beginning in Luke 2:1–7, we have the birth of Christ. Eight days later, in Luke 2:21, we have the dedication of the baby Jesus on the eighth day. From there, we hasten quickly to the tween years of Jesus, which occurs twelve years later. Luke 2:42 recounts the story of Jesus getting lost in the caravan by his parents for an entire day, and they later find Jesus in the temple interfacing with the doctors of religion. Fast-forwarding from there, Jesus matures from middle to late adolescence (Luke 2:52). Finally, Jesus is viewed by God as a full adult (Luke 3:32) at the age of about thirty (Luke 3:21–23) when he is baptized by John in the Jordan River and anointed by the Holy Spirit for ministry. Here you have the comprehensive life of Christ.

However, the key verse of all relative to Christ is Luke 2:52 (NKJV). It states: "And the child grew, and waxed strong in spirit, filled with wisdom: and the grace of God was upon Him." "And Jesus increased in wisdom [mental] stature [physical], and in favour with God [spiritual] and man [social]" (Luke 2:52, KJV). Here is set forth the stages of normality in adolescent development—the physical, the mental, the spiritual, and the social.

Paul succinctly references adolescent development when he writes, "When I was a child, I spake as a child, I understood as a child, I thought as a child: but when I became a man, I put away childish *things*" (1 Cor. 13:11). The Apostle Paul makes it clear that there is a transitional change in the transformation process from childhood to manhood, which is in essence stating that there are stages of development. Paul behaved one way as a child, but he behaved differently as a man.

The Gospel writer John seems to suggest that once a young man reaches maturity, he is capable of much. "I write unto you, little children, because *your* sins are forgiven you for his name's sake. I write unto you, fathers, because ye have known him that is from the beginning. I write unto you, young men, because you have overcome the wicked one. I write unto you, little children, because ye have known the Father. I have written unto you, fathers, because ye have known him that is from the beginning. I have written unto you, young men, because ye are strong, and the word of God abideth in you, and ye have overcome the wicked one" (1 John 2:12–14). Scripture emphasizes three states of development: childhood, young manhood (adolescence), and manhood.

Training and letting go appears to be difficult for parents, but at the same time, it is a very healthy theme in scripture. "Hear, O my son, and receive my sayings; and the years of thy life shall be many. I have taught thee in the way of wisdom; I have led thee in right paths. When thou goest thy steps shall not be straitened; and when thou runnest, thou shalt not stumble. Take fast hold of instruction; let *her* not go: keep her; for she *is* thy life. Enter not into the path of the wicked, and go not in the way of evil *men*. Avoid it, pass not by it, turn from it, and pass away" (Prov. 4:10–15). Solomon, the writer, is in essence stating there is a time for training, then there is a time to let go. Solomon further states, "Train up a child in the way he should go: and when he is old, he will not depart from it" (Prov. 22:6).

The Prodigal Son

In the story of the Prodigal Son, recorded in the Gospel Luke (Luke 15:11–32), where the son decided to leave home from under his fathers care, full maturity—and I say that with caution—for the prodigal son was reached only when he returned home after lessons of life were forced upon him. He actually grew up emotionally when feeding the detested hogs that he was forbidden to touch as a child. Many a sermon has been preached on the prodigal life of the Jewish adolescent who decided to get an early start in life while not fully prepared mentally, spiritually, or emotionally. His experience is a written testimony on what an adolescent should not do—place selfish interest above the known will of God. Ellen G. White's comments speak to this boldly:

> The Bible tells of men who "professing themselves to be wise" "became fools" (Rom. 1:22); and this is the history of the young man of the parable. The wealth which he has selfishly claimed from his father he squanders upon harlots. The treasure of his young manhood is wasted. The precious years of life, the strength of intellect, the bright visions of youth, the spiritual aspirations—all are consumed in the fires of lust. A great famine arises, he begins to be in want, and he joins himself to a citizen of the country, who sends him into the field to feed swine. To a Jew this was the most menial and degrading of employments. The youth who has boasted of his liberty, now finds himself a slave. He is in the worst of bondage—"holden with the cords of his sins" (Prov. 5:22). The glitter and tinsel that enticed him have disappeared, and he feels the burden of his chain. Sitting upon the ground in that desolate and famine-stricken land, with no companions but the swine, he is fain to fill himself with the husks on which the beasts are fed. Of the gay companions who flocked about him in his prosperous days and ate and drank at his expense, there is not one left to befriend him. Where now is his riotous joy? Stilling his conscience, benumbing his sensibilities, he thought himself happy; but now, with money spent, with hunger unsatisfied, with pride humbled, with his moral nature dwarfed, with his will weak and untrustworthy, with his finer feelings seemingly dead, he is the most wretched of mortals. What a picture here of the sinner's [young man's] state![35]

Joseph

When we consider Joseph, the favorite Son of Jacob, who was despised and sold into slavery by his brothers (Gen. 37), Joseph reached maturity through a quick experience en route to Egypt after being sold as a slave.

---

[35] Ellen White, *Christ Object Lessons,* 200.

Joseph, as we know, was a daddy's boy who was loved more by his father Jacob than the other eleven brothers. When Joseph received the coat of many colors from Jacob, it was a token given to him in love. But the key to Joseph's quick maturity, unlike the prodigal son, was that everything Joseph had learned as a child about his father's God came to mind by spiritual recall. Joseph's mind was garrisoned with the word of God.

The lessons Joseph learned in his youth from Jacob—to have a firm trust in God and know the precious evidences of His loving-kindness and unceasing care—were the very lessons he needed in his exile among the idolatrous Egyptians. Even under the severest trial when approached by Potipher's wife, Joseph looked to his God, whom he had learned to trust from the time he was a child. Had the principles and example of Jacob been of an opposite character, the Holy Spirit would never have traced upon the pages in the Word of God the sacred history the story of integrity and virtue that comes forth in the character of Joseph. The early impressions made upon his mind garrisoned his heart in the hour of fierce temptation and led him to exclaim, "how then can I do this great wickedness, and sin against God?" (Gen. 39:9).

Samson

Unfortunately, with Samson maturity came by means of a very difficult lesson. The life of youthful Samson can be summed up in this text: "For he that soweth to his flesh shall of the flesh reap corruption; but he that soweth to the Spirit shall of the Spirit reap life everlasting" (Gal. 6:8).

Few temptations are more dangerous or more fatal to the adolescent than the temptation of sensuality. However, sensuality, when yielded to, will prove to bring ruin to the soul and body for eternity. The welfare of Samson's entire future was suspended upon the decision of a moment.

Consider Joseph for a moment when Potipher's wife approached him with the temptation of sensuality; instead of yielding to her advances, Joseph trusted calmly in God, looking to Heaven for help, slipped off his outer garment when she grabbed him, leaving it in the hands of the temptress. With much spiritual resolve, Joseph determined within himself to forego the sin of sensuality. Joseph exclaimed in her presence, "How can I do this great wickedness, and sin against God?"

When Samson was in peril, he had the same source of strength to depend on as Joseph had, but instead of taking hold of the strength of God, he permitted the passions of adolescence, or that "tinderbox" of sexual emotions, to have full sway. His reasoning powers were perverted, and his morals were corrupted. Keep in mind that God called Samson to a position of great responsibility, honor, and usefulness to deliver his people, but Samson first needed to learn to govern himself by learning to obey the laws of God. Samson, under temptations that he had brought upon himself, gave loose rein to evil passion. The path he entered upon led to his shame and resulted in his death. Many debate over the fact that Samson committed suicide. However, it is my belief that Samson's last prayer was one of deliverance, eventually fulfilling the known will of God. But why did it have to take Samson a lifetime to learn this vital lesson?

When studying biblical examples, I tend to liken adolescence to a seasonal change—a seasonal change in the life of the developing youth that can sometimes bring unpredictable weather. It's a stage of developmental transformation that parents sometimes think will never come to an end. Parents can help the developing adolescent by sharing their successes and failures. With prayer, fasting, patience, and guidance on behalf of the adults in the adolescent's life, proper adolescent development can certainly be accomplished.

CHAPTER THREE

CULTURE AND THE ADOLESCENT

Definition of Culture

The term *culture* is used rather loosely in various settings today. Social scientists define culture as the sum total of the beliefs, accomplishments, and behavior patterns of a particular group of people acquired by members of the group through social learning and sometimes transmitted from one generation to another. John H. Bodley, Chair of the Department of Anthropology at Washington State University, defines culture as a society and its way of life or in reference to human culture as a whole.[36] When referring to adolescents (youths between twelve and twenty-three), we refer to this particular group of individuals as the "teen culture," which is a part of a defined society. Writers sometime refer to this group of teens in the secular sense as the "pop" or "MTV" culture. Christian youth, on the other hand, because of their teachings and philosophical beliefs, are classed as an "adolescent subculture" that is a part of the dominant society.

Biblical Definition of Culture

The Bible does not philosophically define the term *culture*. In scripture, there are no direct references to or mentions of the term. However, you will discover the most prevalent term used by Jesus closely akin to culture would be the term *world*.

To get an understanding of Jesus' view of the term *culture*, all one has to do is read the Gospel of John. This term *world* surfaces eighty times in the

---

[36] John Bodley, *Cultural Anthropology*, 75.

Gospel of John, while it only appears fifteen times throughout the other Gospels. John uses the word *world* (or society of men) particularly when referring to the civilized world[37] and referencing society or culture. John's potent use of the term *world* is suggestive of a society that is diametrically opposed to God and Truth, so John presents Jesus as the Son of God who embraces and confronts culture with truth.

There are several suggested meanings attached to the term *world* in the scripture: A more common meaning used by the Gospel writer John is *kosmos.* The word kosmos literally means "adorning" or "artificial covering," from which we get the word *cosmetics,* which means in essence superficial covering. A second meaning is "the (orderly) universe," or *oikoumeneu,* meaning "the inhabited earth," "mankind," or "the civilized world."[38] It is obvious that in any setting, context determines the usage of the terms. In this context, it is obvious that we are referring to *oikoumeneu*—the civilized world or humanity.

A few references to substantiate this. John seeth Jesus coming unto him, and saith "Behold the Lamb of God, which taketh away the sins of the world" (John 1:29). John 1:10 says, "He was in the *world,* and the *world* was made by him, and the *world* knew him not" (emphasis added). A more familiar text is John 3:16–19:

> For God so loved the world, that he gave his only begotten Son, that whosoever believeth in him should not perish, but have everlasting life. For God sent not his Son into the world to condemn the world; but that the world through him might be saved. He that believeth on him is not condemned: but he that believeth not is condemned already, because he hath not believed in the name of the only begotten Son of God. And this is the condemnation, that light is come into the world, and men loved darkness rather than light, because their deeds were evil.

---

[37] Francis D. Nichol, "John" Vol. 5 of The Seventh-day Adventist Bible Commentary,(Maryland: Review and Herald Publishing Association, 1980), 900.

[38] *"oikoumeneu."* Seventh-day Adventist Bible Dictionary, Hagerstown: Review and Herald Publishing Association, 1980.

1 John 2:15–16 is another familiar text:

> Love not the world, neither the *things* that are in the world. If
> any *man* love the world, the love of the Father is not in him.
> For all that is in the world, the lust of the flesh, and the lust
> of the eyes, and the pride of life, is not of the Father, but is of
> the world.

It is clear in 1 John 2:15–16 "the world" that Christ refers to here
is "kosmos," "artificial adorning," or "coverings," suggestive of sinful
customs, and mores of men and women in society. It is not a theological
discussion between the worlds of animate and inanimate objects that 1
John 2:15–16 refers, but rather kosmos. Context would suggest that Jesus's
use of the term *world* has to do with human communal existence, where
context determines the meaning. The Gospel writer John uses the term
world interchangeably between its two meanings depending on its context.
With this in mind, Christ's use of the term certainly demonstrates that the
world is indeed a sinful place with a compelling sinful power that can and
should be resisted with spiritual resolve. It is clear in John 17:11-12 that
Christ's prayer is for those who are a part of an evil culture.

"And *now* I am no more in the world, but these are in the world, and
I come to thee. Holy Father, keep through thine own name those whom
thou hast given me, that they may be one, as we *are*. While I was with
them in the world, I kept them in thy name: *those* that thou gavest me
I have kept, and none of them is lost, but the son of perdition; that the
scripture might be fulfilled."

Adolescence and Culture

I have discovered through research, experience, and observation that
culture can be a compelling force, not just for the Christian adolescent but
for any adolescent. Everyone wants to be homogeneous—wanting to fit
somewhere. Choices in hairstyles, dress, music, language, and posturing
are in some ways a reflection of fitting not just for teens but also for adults.
Finding that spot where you fit is sometimes difficult and may only come
with life's experiences. No one wants to be considered strange or odd in
today's culture, and this can be a driving force for wanting to assimilate.

Wanting to fit and be accepted by the dominant group or the majority of society can have a profound effect upon the developing adolescent. Not being accepted as a part of the "in" crowd basically places the teen as unpopular among her peer group.

There is a tendency by some adolescent counselors to criticize this need of wanting to assimilate and be accepted by others. However, this basic need of socialization or wanting to be a part is common in all of humanity. God placed in man the need of community. At creation man was surrounded with a perfect world, fulfilling all his necessary domestic needs except one—loneliness.

When God looked at Adam initially, loneliness was the first thing that God's eye named "not good" with someone who was a reflection of Himself. Loneliness and isolation are contradictions to the purpose in God's creative act. God made man to be with a significant other, a female counterpart, thus creating the marriage institution. When God said of humanity that "*It is* not good that the man should be alone" (Gen. 2:18), He meant it physically, emotionally, spiritually, and *socially*.

Adam and Eve were given to each other in part to fill that social vacuum. It is not my intent to hammer away at marriage; however, adolescents also express in various ways the need to fill that social emptiness. Loneliness was never something God had in mind for any of His creative beings. We were created to coexist not only with a significant other but also to coexist within the context of a community. I have discovered that the institution of the church can tremendously decrease the need for or lack of community for adolescents through the programs it provides, which we will discuss at length in a later chapter.

Adolescents at each stage of development feel this need for shared community. There are basically two levels of shared fellowship that adolescents experience. First, boys want to be accepted by their male counterparts, just as much as females want to be accepted by their female counterparts. Within these adolescent circles, you will discover the hierarchal post of leader versus follower. The question that exists with most is, who will emerge as a leader and who will emerge as a follower. Most parents prefer that their children become leaders over followers. As a counselor, I would encourage adolescents to be more concerned with thinking, which is essential to develop the God-given gift of positive decision making. As adolescents develop, moving from high school to college, the college years tend to influence critical thinking tremendously.

A second level where adolescents tend to share the need of acceptance or community is with the opposite sex. As development and growth take place beyond the tween years of ten to twelve, teens want to be accepted by the opposite sex, thus beginning to sense and feel that higher need of their heterosexual calling by God. Sometimes the need of acceptance during this period can be compounded or complicated by physiological changes where the adolescent becomes sensitive to his appearance, which some may call the pimple phase. This is sometimes corrected as the adolescent develops physically.

Unfortunately, adolescents sometimes make immoral decisions in order to become popular and to fulfill their desires to fit in one of the popular peer groups. Teens can get caught up in this cycle of peer acceptance and unacceptable behaviors when there are basically no strong mentors or examples to follow or bond with. Again, the church can be a tremendous help through the programs it provides during this period in adolescents' lives.

CHAPTER FOUR

The Adolescent's Real Problem

Nature's Domination

This chapter clarifies the adolescent's basic problem. I can go further and say it details the human social problem. It's really an issue of reversal. Why do adolescents rebel or express negative behaviors? The answer is quite simple: because it comes naturally. Sin comes with an aggravating character about it.

Let me began with a story that has been a part of my life from childhood. I call this story "the ex-lax factor." Every time I pass the laxative shelf in the pharmacy I smile and move on. For those readers who are unaware, ex-lax is a chocolate-tasting laxative that helps relieve constipation when eaten. As a child, I had a serious problem with lying. My innovative father figured out a way to help bring the problem to the surface. I am the youngest of eight. Needless to say, I was spoiled very early and became a brat who got away with murder, as we often say.

From time to time, slices of cake and goodies would disappear from the kitchen when specific parental instructions had been given to preserve them for a special occasion or church fellowship function. On one such occasion it was a nice slice of German chocolate cake—needless to say, one of my favorites. As usual, Mother would call a council meeting to discover the culprit. With no one stepping up to confess, Dad decided to catch the guilty party on his own.

Dad purchased a bar of ex-lax and a Hershey chocolate bar. After neatly placing the ex-lax in the Hershey wrapper, he put the bar in the refrigerator. After scouting out the territory, I quickly snatched what I believed to be a Hershey bar from the fridge, retreated to my selected hiding place, and quickly consumed the somewhat bitter-tasting chocolate before anyone could discover its disappearance.

Well, within the hour the ex-lax began to do its job—loosening the bowels. Into the night, through the morning hours, and up to early afternoon, I found myself quite often sprinting to the bathroom relieving what I thought was an upset stomach. Instead of Mother and Father questioning us about the missing candy bar, the ex-lax quietly had done its job—exposing my weakness. Did this incident break the lying habit? Not exactly, but it did prove that your "sins will find you out" (Proverbs 28:13) and "whatsoever ye have spoken in darkness shall be heard in the light" (Luke 12:3). But more so, it proved a biblical principle and revealed my true nature from childhood, "they go astray as soon as they be born, speaking lies" (Ps. 58:3).

Scripture tells us that man alone was created in the image of God. Man and woman were created just a little lower than the angels with self-consciousness, personality, rationality, intelligence, creativity, and relationships. God gave man sovereignty over the entire created world and all its vast resources so that man could bring up out of this rich planet immense demonstrations of his marvelous abilities rationally, creatively, and relationally. With the creation of man on day six, the real story of creation actually began. All the rest of creation was only a stage for man to play out the great drama of redemption. All the other creation just provided the backdrop for the history of man.

In Genesis 2, we find the details of the creation. We find the creation of man, the location of man (in the Garden of Eden), the vocation of man (what he was doing), the probation of man (what he was not to do), and the relation of man (when God gave him woman).

Now, all of that is summed up in the first chapter when it says in verse 27: "So God created man in his own image, in the image of God created he him; male and female created he them." Equal in existence but separate in roles and responsibility. When God created them, male and female, He gave them a commission: "subdue it and: have dominion over every living thing that moveth upon the earth" (Gen. 1:28). One aspect of that image, as the passage shows, was authority and rule. Authority, because God wanted man and woman to have power to dominate over the earth, to use their God-given creative administrative qualities, and to preside over and govern the planet. Instructions given to man were simple: subdue and dominate.

Imagine with me: God gave us the freedom to actually control one of the colonies in His vast universe. I have often wondered how much domination and authority God actually gave the first couple. You have to wonder what other limitations God placed on the holy pair beyond the forbidden tree. From my own personal study, it appears the only limitation scripture placed on Adam and Eve was not to wander in the area of the tree of good and evil. Beyond this, they were to dominate and control the earth.

I often wonder if it was possible that man could have spoken and nature itself would have become obedient to the command of the holy pair. Was it possible that Adam and Eve could have commanded the fowls to appear or just lift their hand and birds readily would come and land on their fingers. Was it possible that man may have had the magical touch of sensation, and by the touch of Adam's finger, the hibiscus would have automatically opened? Or, by just passing, the flower would have sensed his presence and opened, giving off rich scents pleasing to his olfactory nerves? How much domination, authority, and power did God give man? We can only imagine. Man was upright; he was given noble traits of character with absolutely no bias toward evil. God endowed Adam and Eve with high intellectual powers, with the strongest possible inducements to be true to their allegiance to God.

While they remained true to God, Adam and his companion were to rule over the earth. Unlimited control was given them over every living thing. The lion and the lamb sported peacefully around the holy pair, lying at their feet and bringing them joy. Birds flittered about without fear as their glad songs ascended to the praise of the created pair and their Creator. Adam and Eve united with the rest of creation to offer thanksgiving to the Father and His son.

The words *subdue* and *dominate* are not tame words; instead, they are strong, commanding terms given by God to man, suggesting that he "take control." When Adam and Even spoke, nature willingly obeyed, falling in line with the directives of their commanding officers. Not only was man to dominate and control, but man was to reflect the rule of God, which was a righteous rulership with a kingly authority. Adam's dominion was a derived dominion in that God was at man's disposal when needed. If an issue surfaced, God was at their ready access. There was a natural affinity between the Creator and the created.

When Adam and Eve sinned against God, they were without excuse. The act of sin brought a complete reversal of man's fortunes. Sin within Eden's parameters was inexplicable. God was at their daily exposure; He sported with them in the cool of the day daily. Angels not only trailed them, but they were at their beck and call. Adam and Eve were left without excuse for their actions. Nevertheless, the act of sin was committed, and they were expelled from Eden with its entrance guarded by angels with flaming swords to prevent them from reentering. The day of sin for Adam and Eve was an unforgettable day; it was explained in the terms of paradise lost.

Again, with this act, a reversal of man's fortunes took place. Sin overturned and rearranged the governing powers of the created pair. Sin disrupted the location of man; they were escorted from Eden in the presence of God. Sin disrupted the vocation of man; they now had to labor by the sweat of their brow. Sin disrupted the probation of man; they went far beyond their parameters. Most of all, sin disrupted the relationship of man. Before sin, Adam and Eve were to dominate and rule together, with Adam assuming the leadership and Eve serving the role of help-meet. (Gen. 2:18–25). After sin, crisis sets in; the command was given by God for man to rule over his counterpart. Cain kills his brother Abel, leaving the first family in complete disarray. Had it not been for Jesus stepping in and filling the gap, death would be inevitable for man eternally separated from God.

To add to this sin madness, the earth became an anathema, cursed, banned, and alienated as a separate continent in God's universe, exiled from the community fellowship of other worlds. Is it a wonder why barriers are erected between cultures and communication problems exist among people today? Sin breathes division, discord, and death. Again, this is the aggravating nature of sin.

When Adam sinned, God asked the profound question, "Adam, where are you?" Adam's kingship and domination was sacrificed, and to this day, he has not fully regained it and will not until the Second Coming of Christ. Until then, man has to fight for his authority. This struggle also relates to the human family, which also manifested when brother killed brother.

After sin, man could no longer dominate and subdue the earth; now the earth dominates and subdues man. Man and woman no longer had unlimited control over their environment; their environment now controls them. Nature was thrown into reverse. Nature, which at one time was controlled by man, now kicks and bites back, bringing forth thorn and thistle. The animals that were named by man are no longer man's friend but now run in terror, rebelling against the once holy pair.

Adam and Eve, who at one time were awakened by the alarm of the morning songs of birds, no longer do animals obey their beckon call, they now flee in terror from their earthly commanders and chiefs. Ellen G. White, a leading female author, writes:

> Under the curse of sin all nature was to witness to man of the character and results of rebellion against God. When God made man He made him to rule over the earth and all living creatures. So long as Adam remained loyal to Heaven, all nature was in subjection to him. But when he rebelled against the divine law of God, the inferior creatures were in rebellion against his rule.[39]

Adam and Eve were given the command to maintain and dress the Garden, to trim and keep it orderly. Now when they go to dress and keep it, nature kicks back with hard rock and forbidden soil that sometimes produce tainted or spoiled fruit. Instead of sweet grapes, you get tart grapes and rotten apples. Nature kicks back. Man no longer pets the dog; now the dog bites back. By the sweat of his brow, man has to toil against the elements of the earth in order to eke out his existence. More importantly, childbirth was intended to be a shared experience of joy for Adam and Eve, free of pain, but after sin, nature kicked back, and childbirth became a very painful experience.

Today, as a result of the change that sin brought about, the home, where man was chosen to reign as leader and patriarch of the family, there seems to have taken place a role reversal where matriarchal dominance now comes into play. Divinely prescribed roles that were given Adam and Eve at creation have become confused; children and adolescents no longer readily obey, but are at times reluctant and rebellious to follow parental directives. This sometimes leads to open rebellion in the home, all as result of the entrance of sin.

---

[39] Ellen White, *Patriarchs and Prophets*, 60.

This reluctance to obey finds its rebellious openness when Cain kills his brother Abel. Later, this behavior is repeated when Ham disrespects his father Noah by laughingly looking upon his father's nakedness when in a drunken stupor, when David has to flee his son Absalom for fear of his own life, and when Eli's two sons, Hophni and Phineas, show him irreverence. This is also illustrated by the story Jesus tells so vividly known as the Prodigal Son. There are times, as in the case of Samson, when parents have done their best, but there is still no guarantee that the adolescent will not rebel. The word of God states: "it shall not return unto me void" (Isa. 55:11).

Sin brought the reversal of man's rule over the earth in nature, in himself, and, most importantly, in the family unit, which explains most of the dysfunction in society, including why teens rebel. Therefore, in order to survive socially, man has to fight for existence as he assumes his leadship position with family dysfunction. This is man's biggest problem, which explains why so much turmoil exists in the home. A reversal of man's nature has taken place where all that he once controlled kicks back, aggravating the human race. Is it a wonder why man has difficulty overcoming issues in the flesh? It is because his personal nature kicks back. As humanity, we must realize that the power of evil will not yield the conflict without a struggle.

Before sin, man had one nature—a blameless, righteousness nature. Since the onslaught of sin, we have a dual nature—good and evil—carrying on a duel, so to speak, within us; where each is attempting to subdue and dominate the other. The Bible explains it best: "For we wrestle not against flesh and blood, but against principalities, against powers, against the rulers of the darkness of this world, against spiritual wickedness in high *places*" (Eph. 6:12). This creates mixed emotions, depression, and bipolarity within the human family. The Bible describes it best as the carnal man, or the fleshly man, at war with the spiritual man. One is trying to dominate and subdue the other. There is a turf war, a battle for the mind, two natures contending to subdue and dominate each other.

The Bible says of children, "they go astray as soon as they be born, speaking lies" (Ps. 58:3). Children are in rebellion from birth, and this rebellion manifests itself openly in adolescence. One story that vividly illustrates this moral sadness and social dysfunction is the birthing process of Jacob and Esau. Upon exiting the womb, Jacob (who was given the name "heel grabber") latched on to his brother's heel, only to carry this feud further with Jacob hating and wanting to kill his brother Esau. Even after coming together and settling their differences, their posterity later reignites this family feud carrying on family and social dysfunction.

In 2011, while attending a summit for depression recovery, the speaker listed suicide as the third leading cause of death among youth during the ages of ten to twenty-four—the adolescent period.[40] Research now substantiates that the religion of Christ can be of tremendous help during this time as a way to help adolescents cope and deal with emotions of hopelessness. Because man's nature is in reverse where carnal temptations of sensuality have control over the rational mind controlling the body, the adolescents source of strength can only come from without, through the religion Christ Jesus. The indwelling Christ, by His Spirit, is the only source that can return humanity back to its true status of rightness. However, man cannot win this struggle without a fight. So what is the adolescent and human problem? Nature's domination.

Biblical Change: What Is It?

There is a concept that has been circulating for years that in essence states that all God has to do is wave His magic wand, and change will come for the Christian. While this may be an oversimplification of the process, there is no change in the life of the child of God without a struggle. However, where help is needed, help is available.

Let me commence this topic with a couple of scriptures. Jeremiah 13:23 states, "Can the Ethiopian change his skin, or the leopard his spots? *then* may ye also do good, that are accustomed to do evil." Luke 11:13 states, "If ye then, being evil, know how to give good gifts unto your children: how much more shall *your* heavenly Father give the Holy Spirit to them that ask him?"

Jeremiah (a.k.a. the weeping prophet) was referring to the Cushites, a people from the upper Nile who the Bible describes as smooth, dark-skinned people (Gen. 10:6) from Ethiopia. They were not unfamiliar with the people of Judah (Jer. 38:10). However, the figure vividly impresses the sad truth that the sin of the people of Judah was so firmly fixed that

---

[40] Nedley, Neil. "Depression Recovery Seminar." Youth Presentation. Dallas, Texas. January 8, 2010

they were not able of themselves to "change" their evil ways. Nothing was left for them but slavery—cords of captivity. So, Jeremiah says, "Can the Ethiopian man change his skin, or the leopard his spots? *then* may ye also do good, that are accustomed to do evil" (Jer. 13:23).

In essence, Jeremiah is saying that it is almost an insurmountable task to change one's way. That's what he meant when he spoke of the people of Judah, who were set in their ways and unwilling to change. John Calvin, in his commentary on Jeremiah 13:23, shares that this passage has been interpreted wrongly as referring to the sinful nature with which men and women are born with. Instead, Calvin insisted it should be understood as a description of "the habit that is contracted by long practice."[41] In other words, habits that you have nurtured—cultivated evil. Careful exegesis, or study, of this passage tends to indicate that Calvin is right because elsewhere Jeremiah makes the same point in another way: "I spake unto thee in thy prosperity; *but* thou saidst, I will not hear. This *hath been* thy manner from thy youth, that thou obeyedst not my voice" (Jer. 22:21).

Jeremiah essentially says that you have been doing this from childhood, so now it's habit. Might I state, biblical change is heaven's goal. The Bible is a book filled with the lives of men and women whose lives were touched and changed by Jesus. Justification and coming to Christ is one thing; however, growing in Christ is another. Sanctification is that road traveled where change takes place in intervals—a little change here and a little change there, on and on until we get to glory. Sanctification is the act and process of being made holy, in the likeness of God.

Let me not mislead you; change can take place in the believer. However, there is no change without a struggle, which is Jeremiah's assertion. Many married couples end up in divorce courts because they find difficulty in making adjustments to their former habits to construct a new way of life that will be different from their two distinct backgrounds. When they come together, realize their individual differences, and see that changing is necessary to make the marriage work, some tend to throw in the white flag of separation.

From another perspective, older persons who have been married for fifty years or more and then suffer the loss of a mate discover that change is inevitable and that it does not come easy. I have known surviving mates

---

41   Francis D. Nichol, vol. 4 of The Seventh-day Adventist Bible Commentary, (Maryland: Review and Herald Publishing Association, 1980), 413

to die not so long afterward, because they could not tolerate the abrupt change that life forces on them after years of happiness. Again, change is necessary but can be difficult.

In the business world, in order to keep pace with progress, companies have to upgrade every eight to ten years in an attempt to stay ahead of the learning curve, because progress and technology are never at a standstill. In order to keep pace and compete, change becomes necessary. If you own a computer that is ten years old, it is obsolete, and upgrading becomes a necessity. If change is necessary in the business world and technology, how much more important is it in the human realm?

When speaking of forgiveness, Jesus is actually discouraging living in a negative past. Why? Because living in the past prevents future change. Realistically thinking, the past no longer exists. It's history. The past can only be dealt with in the present through forgiveness. Scripture speaks of forgetting the past and reaching toward the future. Jesus says to move on from there, change your mantra for living and be happy. Change! We often falter because people tend to recall constantly what has taken place in the past, which prevents future growth. So Jesus says move on toward the future—upgrade.

In Matthew 16:24 Jesus makes a statement that is totally based on discipleship, which sets forth the basis for change in our lives: "Then said Jesus unto his disciples, 'If any *man* will come after me, let him deny himself, and take up his cross, and follow me.'" According to Christ's statement, discipleship is threefold: first, denying self; second, taking up his cross; third, follow Him!

Question: when does a liar cease to be a liar? When he stops lying, or when he starts telling the truth? The answer is when he starts telling the truth—when he changes. When is an adulterer no longer an adulterer? It is when he starts being faithful—change. A constant theme that runs through scripture is "cease to do evil; Learn to do well" (Isa. 1:16–17). Romans 12:21 states, "overcome evil with good." Jesus sets forth the theme for change in Matthew 16:24. I call this in essence the Replacement Theory.

Change is a thread that needles its way through scripture. When you stop doing that which is evil, you learn to do well by replacing it with something good. When you become a child of God, you educate yourself to cease thinking evil by learning to think well. It is the principle of biblical change in the word of God. When God mentions cursing, He always follows with blessings. I have drawn the conclusion from study that personality (who I am) is the sum total of all that one is by nature and nurture. N-a-t-u-r-e, meaning I am born in sin, I am shaped in iniquity, I come here genetically encoded with deep-seated and inherited traits—that's nature, of which I cannot change, which is almost unchangeable (Jer. 13). That's nature.

But then there is nurture. N-u-r-t-u-r-e is that which is acquired, habit. Habit is that which I cultivate. According to Jeremiah, I have been doing it so long that it's a part of me (Jer. 22). Habit is an addiction of what I actually enjoy. You have heard people say, "Oh, I just cannot stop doing that. It's my nature; I have been doing it so long." No, that is what you have nurtured! Don't blame it wrongfully on your nature; blame it on what you have *nurtured* by habit, which becomes another form of addiction.

However, we must keep in mind that God will help you to overcome both inherited and cultivated tendencies to evil—that which what you came here with and that which you have learned. The education process of God is learning that you have to educate yourself. Just like you have cultivated the tendencies to do evil, you can break the addiction to evil by educating yourself to perform and do that which is good. That's sanctified Christianity—growing up in Christ every day by learning to do well. Every day I am educating myself to do better, imitating Jesus, putting off the "old man" as Paul says and putting on the "new man," I am changing my pattern of life and clothing myself with righteousness.

My church offers a health program called CHIP (Complete Health Improvement Program). For those of us who enjoy eating the wrong things, CHIP implements the strategy of countering with eating the right things—putting good in its place. You program your system to eat that which is good. Those who have struggled with dietary issues are very much aware that this can be a tremendous challenge. There is an encoding that happens when you place something better in your system.

Years ago, as a high school student and a developing adolescent, I gave up the idea of eating pork when I began to take my Christianity seriously. I knew I had to go through this dietary change, but I loved that fattening greasy sausage fried deep in oil. The time came for change while I was seated in the school's cafeteria poking at a greasy piece of pork. Knowing that pork is not the best meat that could be consumed, there was an internal struggle going on within me.

While poking and poking and poking, someone came up to me and said, "Man, if you don't want that meat, give it to me. You're just playing with it." As I can recall to this day, that was the last piece of pork I knowingly rejected. However, I did not stop there. I replaced it with beef sausage. Now that I am a vegetarian, I have replaced beef sausage with Gimmie Lean, a type of vegetarian plant-based sausage. When I gave up hamburger, I turned to Vege-burger. When I gave up beef franks, I turned to Vege-franks. I continued putting something better in its place until now; I have absolutely no desire to go back to my old pattern of life. I replaced the old with something new—gracefully. That is sanctified Christianity—growing up in Christ, which will take a lifetime. You move from the bad to the good, from the good to the better, from the better to the best. There is no standstill in Christianity; you are forever changing, forever getting better or moving to higher heights. You are changed by the grace and power of God.

Is this change easy? Was giving up pork easy? Is smoking an easy habit to break? Is gambling an easy addiction to break? No addictions that we have nurtured come with relative ease in quitting. This leads us to step two. Christ's words recorded in Matthew 16:24: "let him deny himself, and take up his cross." Is cross bearing easy? Never! Ask Jesus about that walk from Pilate's judgment through the Via Dolorosa, up Dead Man's hill, to Golgotha. Was it easy, Jesus? What about the six miserable hours spent listening to the taunts and jeers from evil men and demons dispatched in the crowd? Was cross bearing easy? Considering the grave experience, death was alien to Christ. It was something He had never succumbed to, creating within Him the fear of the unknown. Yet, this is the cross He had to bear.

While contending with the Father in the Garden of Gethsemane, Christ prayed, "Father … let this cup pass from me" (Matt. 26:39). Cross bearing was not an easy task for Christ. Likewise, it will be difficult for us. But scripture further substantiates, "there hath no temptation taken US, God is not, and will not, based on His word, allow any of His children to bear more than what we are able to handle" (1 Cor. 10:13). This means both in nature and what we have 'nurtured.' The cross was not easy for Jesus. Crucifying our addictions will not be an easy task for us, but it will bring victory!

With Christianity, you are changing your addictions from that which is evil to that which is good. Linguists would suggest the antonym of *evil* is *good*. Sanctification is a lifestyle process of change—moving from evil to righteousness. That's biblical change, and you do it by crucifixion—crucifying self! Our problem is that we want change, but we do not want to struggle. We do not want to crucify ourselves. We want the victory, but we do not want the fight. We want to stand and stake the victory flag of Christ in our lives, but we do not want to get down in the trenches, wrestle, and fight. Again, there are three components to the text: 1) deny self, 2) take up your cross, and 3) follow me (Christ).

Before you can follow Christ, you have to take up your cross. There are some sacrifices that must be made if victory is to be experienced. There are challenges we must take on, sins we must let go of, give up, and overcome in order to gain the victory. It's a fight that you must decide to engage in and take on, because when you decide to follow Jesus, your nature (that which you are born with) and that which you have nurtured (or cultivated) will not let you go without a struggle. There will be times in the Christian struggle that you may have to claw, scratch, fight, go through withdrawals, and experience cold sweats, chills, and hunger pains to overcome, but with Christ, God's grace will assure the struggling sinner victory.

The tenor in the New Testament that writers use for the child of God is fight, strive, deny, and wrestle. Paul engages both military and sportsman vocabulary to let us know that if we want the blessing, we will have to struggle to get it. If we want the victory, we have to struggle to get it. Jesus calls it cross bearing. Christ says "take up your cross," and the change that Christ offers is possible through Him. Whatever change that God requires of any Christian is possible to gain through Christ. The Holy Spirit helps us effect the change. Notice Jeremiah's taunt in the Old Testament. Jeremiah 13:23 says, "Can the Ethiopian change his skin, or the leopard his spots? *then* may ye also do good, that are accustomed to do evil."

Luke 11:13 says, "If ye then, being evil, know how to give good gifts unto your children: how much more shall *your* heavenly Father give the Holy Spirit to them that ask him?"

Luke answers Jeremiah's claim with the assertion of how this biblical change is caused. "If ye then, being evil, know how to give good gifts unto your children: how much more shall *your* heavenly Father give the Holy Spirit to them that ask him?"

The Holy Spirit will help you effect the necessary change or changes. Remember the man who cleaned his house? When he failed to put something in its place, the evil returned tenfold. He put nothing in its place (Matt. 12:43–45). Remember Jacob? After an entire night of wrestling, he knew the blessing would come if he just held on (Gen. 32:24–26). Remember Paul? He prayed that that thorn would be released, and God's answer was, "My Grace is sufficient" (2 Cor. 12:9).

I am what I call a novice golfer. However, I don't know if I will ever claim to be a proficient golfer, which is my goal. I have two sets of clubs (I am embarrassed to say), a hitting net in my backyard, an artificial hitting surface to hit the long ball in my backyard, a lamp in my study made of golf balls, iron bookends of old classic golfers with the short stick, four CDs on how to learn the game, two pairs of golfing shoes, and two golfing posters suspended from walls in my home and garage. If, per chance, you walked in my house, you would think that I am shooting low scores and am able to teach the game. Not so! I have learned or picked up other hobbies—swimming, sailing, skiing (both water and snow), snowboarding, and scuba—with fair ease. But golfing? Well, that's another story! It is one game I wished I had never taken up, but I do not want to appear as if I've been defeated by the game. When confronting the ball on the tee now, I pray, "Lord, help me to strike this ball right." No one knows the level of difficulty except another golfer, because the game can be very humbling. So it is with the Christian walk.

God's Solution to the Adolescent's Problem: An Ever-Present God

I could not write this book without the assistance of the Holy Spirit, and we cannot live successfully apart from the Spirit's leading in our lives as Christians. The Holy Spirit is vital to the Christian's sustenance.

Upon meeting my intended wife-to-be, my sister, who knows me very well, shared something with my fiancée in private. She only shared it with me later. She said, "I never worry about Winston. He always makes good decisions." I was stunned to hear it, but knowing my source of strength, I can understand. Early during my adolescence, I privately began to depend heavily upon God. I was not precocious spiritually but very much aware of my humanity, which forced this dependence on God. When it comes to the gospel, we discover that the gospel is the power of God and can change a sinner's disposition so that he starts acting contrary to his fallen nature.

Because adolescents are going through various changes, the Holy Spirit helps make the necessary transition from one phase of life to the other richer and smoother. Change can be relatively fluid when the Holy Spirit is leading in the life. Trust me on this one!

The old English term for Holy Spirit is "Holy Ghost," referencing a negative connotation of the spirit world and conjuring in the imagination fear of the unknown. However, when placed in its proper context, Holy Spirit suggests the idea of a "personal comforter" with a spiritual emphasis. Jesus Christ describes the coming of the Holy Spirit as the coming of the Comforter.

> And I will pray the Father, and he shall give you another Comforter, that he may abide with you forever; *Even* the Spirit of truth. (John 14:16–17)

> But the Comforter, which is the Holy Ghost, whom the Father will send in my name, he shall teach you all *things*, and bring all *things* to your remembrance, *whatsoever* I have said unto you. (John 14:26)

> But when the Comforter is come, whom I will send unto you from the Father, *even* the Spirit of truth, which proceedeth from the Father, he shall testify of me. (John 15:26)

> Nevertheless I tell you the truth; It is expedient for you that I go away: for if I go not away, the Comforter will not come unto you; but if I depart, I will send him unto you. (John 16:7)

Comforter here is the given name for Holy Spirit in the sense of companionship. When Adam selectively named the animals he noticed male and female. Upon completion of the naming of the animal kingdom, there was no female counterpart for Adam. God caused a deep sleep to fall on Adam, removed a rib from Adam's side, and created Eve, making her "bone of my bones, and flesh of my flesh" (Gen. 2:23). Eve became Adam's companion, dispelling the sense of loneliness.

In likeness, when the Holy Spirit comes into the life of the child of God, He becomes the voice of God speaking to man as a companion bringing a sense of comfort and security. Granted, as long as the disciples had Christ at their side, there was no fear and no need for a Comforter. Jesus was their companion and comforter. For three and a half years, Christ had labored consistently with the disciples at His side. Day in and day out, they witnessed an everyday human Jesus. Hour by hour, minute by minute, unfolding before their eyes, the disciples saw and felt in person the very essence of God at their side.

Christ was the Holy Spirit, or the voice of God, clothed in flesh twenty-four hours a day for three and a half years. Sleeping at Christ's side, eating at the same table, the disciples were eyewitnesses of His high moments and the painful moments. When pouring out His soul in the Garden of Gethsemane, they were there. At the graveside of Lazarus, they saw a weeping and sorrowful Jesus. With His commanding dispatch and authority, they witnessed demons exorcised and angry storms silenced at His command. Bystanders watched and listened as Christ dispatched the so-called experts in law. In every circle of life, the disciples witnessed, heard, and felt an everyday Jesus.

They were there every day with Christ by their sides, walking, talking, sleeping, eating, rubbing shoulders with, hobnobbing with, and attending social gatherings beside the bona fide, living, warm-blooded Christ. It is said of John, the beloved, the writer of the fourth Gospel, that he was even more blessed. John was the privileged disciple to rest his head in the bosom of Jesus at the Passover Supper. How much closer can one get to the Son of God?

Imagine with me: I picture Christ by the lakeside and in other settings telling stories of the kingdom. Children climb into the very lap of Christ, who, in essence, is God in flesh. They rest their heads against His bosom and are lulled to sleep by the vibration of His beating heart. This was the everyday Jesus.

The disciples of Christ witnessed lame men walk, diseased women healed, and blind men given sight. They watched him provide food for the multitudes by the multiplication of five loaves and two fish. There were miracles every day. Before the story ends, they would witness an arrest and see Him falsely accused, beaten mercilessly like an animal, ridiculed by the crowd, and placed on a cross. All the while, demons in human form cackled and laughed, shouting their cruel invectives as the Son of God died like a common criminal for the sins of men. This was the everyday Jesus the disciples would witness. In every aspect of life, Christ followers would watch as He would be buried in a borrowed grave, come back from the dead, walk though the doors, and finally ascend to glory. The disciples had a hands-on learning experience every day, every moment of their lives.

However, in John 14, Jesus had begun to prepare the disciples for His departure when He would move from the physical Jesus to a spiritual Jesus. A new era of the existence of God would take place. Christ was preparing them for His move from the physical era to the spiritual era. When we think about it, God has always been with humanity. He walked and talked with Adam and Eve in the cool of the Garden. At Babylon, God said, "Let us go down" (Gen. 11:7). In the pillar of fire, it was Jesus who led the way and who kept the Israelites warm in the desert night as they fought off beasts and creatures of the night. It was Jesus in the cloud by day as the Israelites traveled beneath the seething Near Eastern sun, providing them shelter from the heat (Exod. 13:22).

When the Israelites got too hot and were in need of water, Christ gave them water from a hot desert rock that Moses struck. The Bible tells us that rock was Jesus (1 Cor. 10:4). They were fed bread from heaven every day. Christ took them by the hand and led the Children of Israel to the Promised Land. At no point and time in their existence, as far as history can recall, had God ever left or forsaken man. At humanity's darkest hour, God manifests His presence; never has God ever left humanity without a companion.

As Christ prepared to make a transition and leave Earth for Heaven, moving from one state of existence to another and ushering in a new era, He introduced the disciples to a brand of Himself but in a different form. And that was the person of the Holy Spirit, offering them reassurance that "I will not leave you comfortless" (John 14:18). In John 13:33, Jesus announced His departure using the term of endearment "little children," which was a term a rabbi would use when addressing his pupils. Christ knew He could not accomplish in person what His Spirit could do by its omnipresence. John 14 is a continuation of the conversational sequence Jesus had begun in John 13:33, encouraging them in love, "love one another; as I have loved you" (John 13:34).

History teaches that we love progress, but we tend to dislike change. The disciples of Christ were no different than humanity today. Resisting passing the baton and the new method of ministry, the disciples could not understand the words of Christ. They failed in principle and theory to understand the work of the Holy Spirit and the coming of the new age. Christ wanted the best for His disciples. He wanted their hearts to be anchored by faith to the heart of God, and the way to accomplish this was through the indwelling power of the Holy Spirit.

John 16:8 states the work of the Holy Spirit: "And when He comes, He will convict people of their sins, urge them to accept the righteousness that is from above and tell them of judgment to come." In regard to sin, it is because men do not believe in Christ. In regard to righteousness, it is because He was going to the Father. And in regard to the judgment, it is because the Prince of this world now stood condemned. Christ was reminding them that He was leaving and that a Comforter would come in His stead, not leaving them without a witness of God.

Remember the Words of Christ: "I will never leave you, no never leave you" (Greek Translation: John 14:18).[42] Again, Christ is moving from personal existence to a spiritual existence, and the selective term in use by John is *Comforter,* because what will happen to the followers of Christ in the days to come will prove the need of a Comforter. The original Greek rendering of Holy Spirit is *parakletos,* which translated means "called to one side." It is derived from the compound word *para* ("one side" or "half," from which we derive paralysis) and *kletos* ("called to," coming from the term *kaleo* or "to call"). Putting these two together like any good grammarian, you come to understand that the Comforter, or the Holy Spirit, is called by God to be at the side of every believer in a state of spiritual existence. The sentence taken from the original rendering, "I will never leave you, no, never, ever, leave you." Christ knew that His disciples would need this assurance. As Eve was placed at Adam's side to comfort and cheer him and serve as a helpmate, and as Christ was at the side of the His disciples, so the Comforter comes to the side of the believer. When you actually think about it, the disciples were juvenile in their understanding and thinking when it came to the Holy Spirit's presence until after the Holy Spirit fell in large portion in Acts 2.

---

42 Greek original translation.

Several years ago, I experienced an eight-year separation and divorce after a sixteen-year marriage. I discovered it wasn't so much the need of sexual intimacy that began to tear away at my soul, but instead, it was the need for companionship. While driving my four-wheel drive along on the back roads of the Sandia Mountains on a snowy day in New Mexico, reality began to hit home. I stumbled upon a scenic view where nature played its magic upon my senses. Far away from the artificial sounds of society, I could hear snowflakes falling and blanketing the earth and see water breaking rock, giving a sense of the presence of God in nature. Hastily, I turned to the passenger seat to share the Kodak moment only to find an empty seat.

Momentarily, I recognized and understood that as a child of God, I was not created to walk and appreciate such scenes of nature alone. I was created for companionship, spiritually, mentally, physically, and socially. As with all of Christ's followers, I was not created to be alone. Instead, we were created for companionship with our Creator. As the statement goes, no man is an island, and no man stands alone. That is indeed a truism.

In Revelation, John says the church is now the bride of Christ. Christ is married to his church in the person of the Holy Spirit. We are now living the age or era of spiritual companionship with God. Through the abiding presence of the Spirit, we who are followers of Christ are to witness an everyday Jesus. Through the Spirit's presence, adolescents, as well as adult believers, are to experience a walking, talking, breathing, bona fide, warm-blooded Christ who rubs shoulders and hobnobs with His followers. Christ, though His Spirit, is wedded to us and gives us a sense of security. "I will never leave you, no, never, ever, leave you."

The words of Ellen White best describe the Holy Spirit:

> The Holy Spirit is Christ's representative, but divested of the personality of humanity, and independent thereof. Cumbered with humanity, Christ could not be in every place personally. Therefore, it was for their interest that He should go to the Father, and send the Spirit to be His **successor** on earth. No one could then have any advantage because of his location or his personal contact with Christ. By the Spirit the Saviour

would be accessible to all. In this sense He would be nearer to them than if He had not ascended on high.[43]

Further reading would substantiate the following:

> As Christ lived the law in humanity, so we may do if we will take hold of the Strong for strength. But we are not to place the responsibility of our duty upon others, and wait for them to tell us what to do. We cannot depend for counsel upon humanity. The Lord will teach us our duty just as willingly as He will teach somebody else. If we come to Him in faith, He will speak His mysteries to us personally [by means of His spirit].[44]

The Apostle Paul, writing to the Galatians, wrote,

> *This* I say then, Walk in the Spirit, and ye shall not fulfill the lust of the flesh.

> For the flesh lusteth against the Spirit, and the Spirit against the flesh: and these are contrary the one to the other: so that ye cannot do the *things* that ye would.

> But if ye be led of the Spirit, ye are not under the law.

> Now the works of the flesh are manifest, which are *these*; Adultery, fornication, uncleanness, lasciviousness, Idolatry, witchcraft, hatred, variance, emulations, wrath, strife, seditions, heresies, envying, murders, drunkenness, revelling, and such like: of the which I tell you before, as I have also told *you* in time past, that they which do such *things* shall not inherit the kingdom of God. But the fruit of the Spirit is love, joy, peace, longsuffering, gentleness, goodness, faith, Meekness, temperance: against such there is no law. (Gal. 5:16–23)

---

[43]   Ellen White, *Desire of Ages*, 669.
[44]   Ibid., 669.

In Ephesians 5:18, Paul writes: "And be not drunk with wine … but be filled with the Spirit." God has made Himself available to us by giving us His Spirit. Luke 11:13 states, "If ye then being evil, know how to give good gifts unto your children: how much more shall your heavenly Father give the Holy Spirit to them that ask him?"

Jesus gave Judas, as He did with the other disciples, the power to heal the sick. The Spirit of God worked with Judas till darkness set in on His soul and he allowed the devil to move in. When Judas left the Passover meal, the whole ambience of the room changed, because evil was gone and only Jesus was there. But up to that point, the Spirit of God was toiling with Judas to the very end. The Bible says that when Judas walked out, "it was night" (John 13:30). Not only was there physical darkness, but there was a spiritual darkness.

Now let's fast-forward to 90 AD. John the beloved is an old man. He is abandoned on a little isle called Patmos somewhere sequestered in the Aegean Sea, placed in exile away from friends, family, loved ones, and associates and kept from doing the things that he loved. I don't know if Patmos was a place where wild animals hovered and snakes dwelt among rocks, but I also don't think it was some little sunny vacation spot for the Caesar Domitian (the ruler at that time). If that were so, Domitian would have kept it for himself.

Research suggests that Patmos was used for penal purposes, so John was placed there for doing the will of God. But when John wrote, he said, he was "in the Spirit" on the "Lord's Day" (Revelation 1:10).

The Spirit of God came alongside and comforted John in his time of loneliness on Patmos.

John, in the seventh and final letter on the correspondence list of Jesus, is writing to those who exist prior to the coming of Christ, giving a final warning, directly from the throne room of God. The message John bears is a message of rebuke. Yet at the same time, it is a message of comfort.

> I know thy works, that thou art neither cold nor hot: I would thou wert cold or hot. So *then* because thou art lukewarm, and neither cold nor hot, I will spue thee out of my mouth. Because thou sayest, I am rich, and increased with goods, and have need of nothing; and knowest not that thou art wretched, and miserable, and poor, and blind, and naked: I counsel thee to buy of me gold tried in the fire, that thou mayest be rich;

and white raiment, that thou mayest be clothed, and *that* the
shame of thy nakedness do not appear; and anoint thine eyes
with eyesalve, that thou mayest see. As many as I love, I rebuke
and chasten: be zealous therefore, and repent. Behold, I stand
at the door, and knock: if any *man* hear my voice, and open
the door, I will come in to him, and will sup with him, and he
with me. To him that overcometh will I grant to sit with me in
my throne, *even* as I also overcame, and am set down with my
Father in his throne. He that hath an ear, let him hear what the
Spirit saith unto the churches. (Rev. 3:15-20)

The key word in this passage is *sup*. God wants to come, sit down, talk,
associate, and connect with His people. Through the abiding presence of
His Spirit, God has made everything heaven has to offer accessible to us
by the power and presence of His Spirit.

I would like to close this chapter with an experience. Several years
ago, I attended a conference in Orlando, Florida. Not far from Orland
is Cape Canaveral, where shuttle flights are launched. From my hotel
room, I had the privilege of watching one of these man-made crafts defy
gravity after lifting off. Like a child, I stood in awe of technology and
twenty-first-century space travel.

Later, after reading about the flight, I discovered that the payload was
an additional satellite that would be dispatched to orbit Earth, suspended
in space, where it would transmit radio-wave signals to civilian transmitters
called GPS (Global Positioning System) devices. The global positioning
system is a global navigation satellite system (GNSS) developed by the
US Department of Defense and managed by the US Air Force 50th Space
Wing. It is the only fully functional GNSS in the world, can be used
freely, and is often used by civilians—people like me—for navigation
purposes. It uses a constellation of between twenty-four and thirty-two
medium Earth-orbiting satellites that transmit precise radio-wave signals,
which allow GPS receivers to determine their current location, the time,
and their velocity. Its official name is NavStar GPS.

Considering that I am a gadget person, a few years ago my wife
gave me my first handheld gadget, then called a PDA (Personal Digital
Assistant), a.k.a. Palm. Today, the closest equivalent would best be known
as an iPhone. Built into my PDA was TeleNav GPS Navigation software,

which allowed access a radio-wave signal from the GNSS. This signal allows me to find a given location or businesses once I key in the address.

No matter my current location, I can access my time of travel, distance, estimated time of arrival, traffic conditions, and weather from my PDA. When I'm driving, it speaks to me and gives me specific directions. It also allows me to know when I have erred and redirects me back on track. I can do all this from my PDA, yet at the same time, I am unable to see the orbiting satellite, somewhere suspended in space. I know it is there, yet not by sight.

I now walk with my PDA/5G Phone and can access sports, current news, weather, directions, e-mails, bank accounts, etc.—all from one handheld device created by man. And this information is transmitted through a radio-wave signal from a satellite that I cannot see suspended in space. What amazing technological advancement.

We all are familiar with the Christmas story where wise men from the East came in search of the Christ-child guided by a star. These men were Gentiles, men of wealth, philosophers from the educated strata of heathenism. Yet, they were simple enough to follow the known will of God as revealed by scriptures. They studied nature in connection with nature's God. When drawing their conclusions, they filtered all their learning through the word of God.

The magi learned from their studies that the coming of Christ was near and that the whole earth one day would be filled with a knowledge of the Lord. Through their dreams, the Spirit of God was guiding them in search of the newborn Prince. Traveling by day, they were navigating their way through the word of God, searching the prophecies; by night, they were guided by the star. We can conclude that the guiding star that appeared in the night sky could have been, as one author suggests, a distant company of angels. On the other hand, nature, which is also at God's disposal, could also have led these wise men to Bethlehem. Nevertheless, whether an act of nature or angels, who are messengers of God dispatched from the very throne room of God, both were God's GPS signal transmitters guiding the magi to their newborn king.

If, per chance, man can create a handheld device that can guide me from point A to point B through a transmitted radio-wave signal from a satellite orbiting the planet that I cannot see, God can certainly use His Holy Spirit to guide me as He did with the magi.

We can certainly trust the Holy Spirit to be the Comforter to us.

CHAPTER FIVE

THE ADOLESCENT'S HEALTH

And Jesus increased in wisdom and stature, and in favour with
God and man. (Luke 2:52)

I want to briefly return to that rosy theme outside my study window
that I hinted to in my introduction—the velvet whites, the rosy reds,
the girly pinks, and pristine yellows, all in different sizes and color with
distinctive scents. These delicate flowers have been nourished by the soft,
godly morning sun and delicate showers. I must say, a little added muscle
for cultivation and fertilizer help push them toward beauty, full maturity,
and total health. Adolescent development is very similar to that of my rose
plant bed; each adolescent is different in his own distinctive way that need
the support of nurturing adults around them. In this chapter, I want to
consider the adolescent's health.

What is it that contributes to the total well-being of the adolescent?

I grew up in the South. Quite reminiscent are the southern scenes
in the movie *Fried Green Tomatoes,* but far removed in time and culture.
Growing up, our diet was heavily supplemented with the backyard garden
variety—beans, peas, greens, tomatoes, potatoes, squash, corn, and
cucumbers. Fruit, such as plums, wild grapes, melons, and all kinds of
wild berries were free and plenteous. Comparatively speaking, that sounds
like a good diet. All we had to do was gather and eat. Poultry, beef, and
seafood were also considered prime Southern meaty staples. Since then,
I have chosen—for health reasons—to remove the fleshy part of my old
diet, replacing it with a plant-based substitute.

As children and adolescents, my generation did not have the "luxury"
of Nintendo, computers, DVDs, and video games. If so, the games were
of the educational variety and less of the sedentary recreational. Our

recreation basically consisted of outdoor activities or sweaty gyms and swimming pools ventilated by open doors with large fans at the entrance. Seemingly, things have somewhat changed.

My nieces and nephews have become more sedentary in their lifestyle, which is reflected in their size. I can't but say it—they are simply "supersized" kids! I have witnessed three of five kids (close to home) who are overweight, with the two smaller ones yet to reach their full body composition. When visiting home, my sister's kitchen is literally the center of family activity. Because family homes are within close proximity of each other in so-called country living, Grandpa and Grandma's kitchen has become a café where we sit around a country-style table and relish home-cooked meals straight from the pot. No matter the time of day or night, when the grandkids walk through the back door, pretentiously hungry, Grandma obliges with big plates of fries, heavily salted and peppered and with lots of ketchup.

The entertainment of adolescents today consist of downloaded action movies, YouTube, computer games and music downloaded on ipods, ipads etc.; those of the recreational variety rather than educational, and a diet heavily supplemented with fast foods. As I write this, I am sitting in a church member's home peering through the window and watching their seven-year-old nephew race across the drive with a Dr. Pepper braced against his lips. Sitting on the back carport is an ice chest filled with pop, where kids can come and select their choice brand freely. How's that for healthy kids?

Let's not fool ourselves. Briefly reading a magazine I picked up awaiting an appointment, I can agree with Yale scientists and food activists when they conclude we now live in a toxic food environment. Thank God our current president's wife noticed this epidemic and has decided to draw attention to the problem by growing a vegetable garden in the backyard of the White House.

It was brought to my attention by a friend that when you go to the doctor for health tips, in the waiting room you find a magazine titled *Family Doctor: Your Essential Guide to Health and Well-Being* published by the American Academy of Family Physicians. In 2004, the publication was being sent free to the offices of all fifty thousand family doctors in the United States. Within these magazines, you find ads for McDonald's, Dr. Pepper, chocolate pudding, and Oreo cookies. To put it simply, Western society has been inundated with an unhealthy diet, which is now reflected in the Western lifestyle.

Now, just think with me. Adolescence is a time when there is a ten- to twelve-year growth spurt. Adolescence is a time period of the changing of the guard, so to speak, moving from childhood to adulthood. At a time when youth should be feeding and nurturing a developing physical system, the growth processes are actually stunted by their dietary lifestyle choices.

Let's look at some statistical facts. According to the Dr. T. Colin Campbell and Thomas M. Campbell, authors of "*The China Study*,"[45] about 15 percent of America's youth (ages six to nineteen) are overweight. Another 15 percent are at risk of becoming overweight.[46] It can be substantiated that overweight children face a wide range of psychological and social challenges. When dealing with each other, children can be mean-spirited and merciless.

Obese children find it more difficult to make friends and are often thought of as lazy and sloppy. More than likely, they will have behavioral and learning difficulties, and many will suffer from low self-esteem that lasts through adolescence and sometimes well into their adult lives.[47] Young people who are overweight also are highly likely to face a host of medical problems. They often have elevated cholesterol levels, which can be a predictor for any number of deadly diseases. They are more likely to have glucose intolerance and, consequently, diabetes.[48] Type 2 diabetes, formerly seen only in adults, is skyrocketing among adolescents. Elevated blood pressure is nine times more likely to occur among obese kids. Sleep apnea, which can cause neurocognitive problems, is found in one in ten obese children.

A wide variety of bone problems are more common in obese kids. Most importantly, an obese young person is much more likely to be an

---

[45]   T. Campbell, & Thomas M. Campbell, *The China Study* (Dallas: BenbBella Books, Inc, 2006), Oxford University Press, 1990), 113

[46]   C.L. Ogden, C.M Flegal, M.D. Carrol, et al. *Prevalence and trends in overweight among U.S. Children and Adolescence*. JAMA 288 (2002): 1728-1732

[47]   WH. Dietz, "*Health Consequences of Obesity in Youth: Childhood predictors of adult disease.*" Pediatrics 101 (1998): 518-525.

[48]   T. Campbell, & Thomas M. Campbell, *The China Study* (Dallas: BenbBella Books, Inc, 2006), Oxford University Press, 1990), 137

obese adult, greatly increasing the likelihood of lifelong health problems.[49] Type 2 diabetes is the most common form of diabetes accompanied by obesity. As Americans continue to gain weight at the current rate,[50] Type II diabetes increased 33 percent from 1990 to 1998. The surprising thing is that more than 8 percent of American adults are diabetic, and more than 150,000 young people have contracted type 2 diabetes.[51] This translates to 16 million Americans, with one-third completely unaware that they have contracted it. What makes this situation more serious is when our children, at the age of puberty, contract a form of juvenile diabetes that has historically been reserved for adults older than forty. What is going on with the diet of adolescents?

To add to the diabetic problem, the Western struggle with weight is hard to miss. Open a newspaper or a magazine or turn on the radio or TV. You can't miss the weight problem that grips our country. Statistics have proven, according to this same China study, that two of every three adults in America are overweight, and one-third of the adult population is obese.[52] Perhaps you've been in a classroom or on a playground or at any day-care center and seen that it is a fact. By sheer observation, it's clear that America's children have an obesity problem. What appears to be the problem? Lifestyle. What's the solution? A lifestyle change.

Because adolescence is a period of internal and external growth, overall health is of extreme importance for the well-being of the developing youth. Early dietary and eating habits are of extreme importance and should be continued throughout adolescence. Some of the behavioral issues that teachers and social workers encounter can, in part, be traced to lifestyle.

What's the solution to our Western dietary problem? Hans Diehl of the Coronary Health Improvement Program states, "Genetics load the gun; lifestyle pulls the trigger." It's not genetics that's killing us; it's the lifestyle we have chosen to live. I am a saltwater enthusiast. In my home study, I have a synthetic saltwater environment filled with invertebrates (plantlike organisms) that awe the imagination as to how they subsist removed from their natural ocean setting. The color and brightness of my

---

[49]   Ibid., 137.

[50]   Two-thirds of Americans are considered overweight, and more than 15 million Americans have diabetes. One-third of the children are overweight or at risk of becoming overweight.

[51]   Ibid., 175.

[52]   Ibid., 139.

artificial reef, as is with the many roses outside my study window, dazzle the imagination. What I discovered from my saline creation is that for plant and fish life to subsist there must be a healthy balance of proper nutrients, proper sunlight, and healthy water for quality living conditions. If it's needed for a healthy fish environment, what about the developing adolescent?

Let's face it. For the most part, teens are not taught what is best for them theoretically. Diets, for the most part, are modeled by what they are fed from the dinner table passed down by means of tradition—what we were traditionally taught. Although our parents did the best they could with what they had, I can rightfully say as a parent now that it was not always the best.

My son, who is of average size and build, at times thinks his body to be a Sherman tank, for lack of better words, based on what he consumes from my kitchen. Although I realize I cannot police his dietary habits, I can, as a parent, place at his disposal good food for consumption. I intentionally make it very difficult for him to have fast foods from the home refrigerator. Many adolescents fuel their bodies with the popular entrées of engineered fast foods (burgers, fries, pizza, chips, pop, tacos, etc.), which are often not the best means of nourishment. Adolescents often have a knack of leaving the leafy greens and other vegetables on their plates. At church potlucks, when eating among my youthful followers, I have a tendency to look over their shoulders and remind them to "put something green on that plate." I enjoy being the vegetable cop, causing them to have a nutritional guilt trip. Again, genetics load the gun, and lifestyle pulls the trigger.

On the other hand, the key to healthy living for the adolescent is a balanced lifestyle. The balanced lifestyle is the goal. Scripture is very clear "And Jesus increased in wisdom and stature, and in favour with God and man" (Luke 2:52). Christ grew spiritually, mentally, socially, and physically. It was God's intention from the beginning that all His children would prosper. Because of the sin of our fore-parents, Adam and Eve, it was genetically encoded in the bloodline traits that we would be susceptible to ailments, physical deficiencies, evil tendencies, and illnesses, predisposing Christ and the whole of humanity to sin. However, unlike us, "Jesus sinned not."

Before sin, humanity was created with an insurmountable amount of vital force or inborn strength. The antediluvians, who were people living prior to the universal flood of Noah, were considered giants,[53] men of great stature and strength, renowned for their wisdom and skill. The lifespan of man was measured not so much in years but instead in centuries. Adam lived well over nine centuries or nine hundred years.

Before the flood, the antediluvians, as they as they were called, were considered giants in mind and body. The human race for many generations retained much of its early vigor just a few generations removed from Adam, who had access to the Tree of Life. This so-called Tree of Life did exactly what its purpose was, which was to prolong life as they ate of its fruit. The River of Life that ran through Eden and the New Jerusalem was distinctly placed there as a beverage to extend and prolong life.

Considering one of the tallest men today is about 7'5" and weighing close to 300 pounds, to have lived as an antediluvian, that man would have been fifteen to sixteen feet tall, weighing 600-hundred-plus pounds, twice his size and weight today,[54] rather a big man with solid muscle mass and limitless mental capability. Because the antediluvians, were of lofty stature, their thinking capacity far exceeded that of humanity today. Their minds—of equal value to their size—enabled them to perform mathematical and scientific equations employed by computers today. They were simple, everyday equations generally carried out and performed by their giant intellectual ability.

How did they maintain? The nourishment provided by God[55] and given to humankind was taken from trees planted in the midst of the garden. In other words, they were given a plant-based diet. A plant-based diet composed of fruits, grains, nuts, and vegetables[56] prescribed for the human race, creating a wholesome, nutritional balance. God chose to exclude animal products from their diet until after the flood.[57]

As a cohesive unit, mind and body were designed to work together; it is through the intellect that God has chosen to effectively communicate with us by means of the Holy Spirit. When the nutrient-rich foods given

---

[53]   Genesis 6:4.

[54]   Ellen White, *The Story of Redemption*, (Hagerstown: Review and Herald, 1977), 21.

[55]   Genesis 2:8–10.

[56]   Genesis 3.

[57]   Genesis 9:1-5

by God to man are consumed, they strengthen the blood,[58] which in turn feeds the brain, giving allowance for effective communication between man and God and leading to a holistic, balanced lifestyle.

How does all this apply to adolescence? As stated earlier, because adolescence is a transitional and transformational state of development between childhood and adulthood, a balanced lifestyle should be maintained without question.

According to *Health Power*, coauthored by Aileen Ludington, MD, and Hans Diehl, DrHsc, MPH, there are eight natural remedies, which, if followed, will lead to a balanced lifestyle and prolonged life. These natural remedies are nutrition, exercise, water, sunlight, temperance, air, rest, and trust in divine Power,[59] popularly known as NEW START.

The Importance of Proper Nutrition

Like Adam and Eve and many of the antediluvians, there are more than 16 million vegetarians today in the United States alone. Vegetarians are considered healthier and more ecologically sound.[60] The three leading killers in the United States today are heart disease, cancer, and stroke. The average risk of heart disease for a man eating meat, eggs, and dairy products is 45 percent. However, the coronary risk of a vegetarian who leaves off meat, eggs, and dairy products drops to only 4 percent.[61]

An editorial in the *Journal of the American Medical Association* commented on these advantages. It is said, "A total vegetarian diet can prevent up to 90 percent of our strokes and 97 percent of our heart attacks."[62] Going beyond prevention, Dean Ornish has published studies

---

[58]   It should be noted that the biblical mandate given to man is "do not eat the blood" (Gen. 9:4) because the blood is the life. The spiritual application is also appropriate—Jesus shed His blood so that we can have life. Blood equates to life.

[59]   These remedies can easily be remembered as the NEW START (Nutrition Exercise, Water, Sunlight, Temperance, Air, Rest, Trust in Divine Power) program promoted by Ludington and Diehl.

[60]   H. Diehl and D. Ludington, *Health Power: Health by Choice*, Not by Chance(Hagerstown, Review and Herald Publishing, 2000) 181.

[61]   Ibid., 182.

[62]   Ibid., 187.

proving beyond a shadow of a doubt that a very low-fat, vegetarian diet could reverse heart disease in patients scheduled for coronary bypass surgery.[63] As noted earlier, because of our predisposition to sin, genetics load the gun, and lifestyle pulls the trigger. We should medicate ourselves with the proper foods. We must keep in mind that the antediluvians, whose life span was measured in centuries, were sustained by a vegetarian diet.

The Need for Exercise

The facts suggest that we either use it or lose it. Exercise helps us feel good physically and mentally. It strengthens the heart and lowers blood pressure and resting heart rate, protecting the heart and blood vessels and strengthening the bones by helping retain calcium and other minerals. Outdoor exercise is a valuable tool in lifting depression and relieving anxiety and stress. It increases our overall energy and efficiency in all areas of life. It improves circulation, and that makes for clearer minds, better sleep, and faster healing of damaged body areas.

The Importance of Water

It is said if you placed juice and water before animals that react off their instincts, they would consume the water. Just as the Tree of Life was placed in the midst of the Garden of Eden for nourishment, so the River of Life ran through Eden for man as the natural beverage. Most nutritionist recommends a daily consumption of six to eight glasses of water per day.[64] I personally subscribe to the principle of enough water to keep my urine of the clear variety rather than a golden yellow.

Adolescents, as well as the rest of Americans, drink more soft drinks and alcoholic beverages than the daily recommended water consumption. These substitutes force the body to deal with calories and chemicals and can disturb the process of digestion. The body needs water to function

---

[63]   Ibid., 190.
[64]   Ibid., 135.

and be able to properly cleanse the system of toxins. Like oil is to the engine, so is water to the system. It serves as the body's lubricant.

The Need for Sufficient Sunlight

According to Hans Deihl, *Health Power*, sunlight is an efficient germ killer. Proper amounts of sunshine give the skin a healthy glow and help make it smooth and pliable. Sunlight elevates the mood for most people, producing a sense of well-being. Combined with active exercise, sunshine is important in treating depression. With much sunlight, the body is able to manufacture vitamin D by the action of sunlight on the skin. Vitamin D enables the body to pick up calcium from the intestines for use in building healthy bones. Sunlight helps to enhance the immune system, alleviates pain from swollen arthritic joints, relieves certain symptoms of PMS, and lowers cholesterol levels. While there are many positives in getting plenty of sunlight, be careful of overexposure.[65]

Temperance: What Is It?

Dr. Hans Selye states, "the human body—like the tires on a car wears longest when it wears evenly."[66] Another meaning of the word *temperance* is balance. The key for adolescence is balance. It is during the adolescent transitional years that most concentrated sugars are consumed in soft drinks, candy, cakes, and pies, etc. We must remember the key to longevity is a balanced lifestyle. This balance is important for everything we do in life. Too much of anything is not good. Jesus was the most balanced human to ever walk planet Earth. Someone said that "balance is common sense in action." Most people don't die of old age. Instead, we invariably die because one vital part has worn out too early in proportion to the rest of the body.

---

[65]   Ibid., 175.
[66]   Ibid., 130.

Fresh Air: A God Given

When God "breathed into his nostrils the breath of life; and man became a living soul" (Gen. 2:7). Air is the breath of life. We are fully dependent on air for oxygen to operate the powerhouses in our body cells. Air conveys life, vigor, and electrifying energy to every cell in the body. The brain needs air to function properly. Because I am a pastor, a great majority of my time is consumed at the pulpit and seated at my desk. While speaking at one of the many small churches I have pastored, during the morning service, I noticed the children were very irritable and jumpy. I asked the deacons to crack the windows for proper circulation, and within ten minutes, they were more relaxed. There was a need for fresh air.

When air is received through the lungs, the heart sends blood through the entire system. That blood is filled with red blood cells whose hemoglobin picks up fresh oxygen in the lungs and delivers it to every cell in the body. The human body operates on oxygen; this is why ventilation is important in the home, workplace, and school. Bad air and poor breathing habits promote negative emotions like depression and irritability. Little oxygen to the brain causes headaches and chronic feelings of fatigue and exhaustion.

Sufficient Rest

Rest allows the body to renew itself. During this resting time, waste products are removed, repairs are done, enzymes are replenished, and energy is restored. Resting assists in the healing of injuries, infections, and other assaults on the body, including stress and emotional traumas. Rest strengthens the body's immune system, helping protect it from disease. Proper rest can add length to the adolescent's life. It was discovered in a health study that people who regularly slept seven to eight hours each night had lower death rates than those who averaged either less than seven hours or more than eight hours.

Trusting in God: The Need for Divine Power

The very root of health is a relationship with the Divine Creator. Adam and Eve were at their best when they engaged in conversation with God in Eden during the cool of the day. Spiritual growth supplies that missing piece in our lives that can only be filled by our maker. Religion is a way of life that includes who we are, all that we do, our hopes, our aspiration, and each moment of our lives. It would be well for each of us to learn to cultivate spending a thoughtful hour with God each day. The Bible says of Christ: "And in the morning, rising up a great while before day, he went out, and departed into a solitary place, and there prayed."[67] We too must cultivate that same habit. Adolescence is one of the best times to start developing a devotional life.

---

[67]   Mark 1:35.

CHAPTER SIX

Socialization: Modeling, Nurturing, and Teaching

Recently my wife received the standardized scores for our two-teacher school. As expected, quite a number of her students performed at peak level. The few who did not do well were a smaller number compared to those who did perform at their best. The overall scores ranked in the eightieth percentile range. As the pastor of this small church and school, I was quite elated, evoking a personal response of "not bad."

However, my next question was key. What contributed to their success? My wife's answer was quick and to the point. "Consistency," she said. Consistency? Yes, consistency. When parents work with teachers, there is guaranteed success. "Furthermore," she added, "those that did well, I have had the opportunity of working with them from pre-K to where they are presently." Believe it or not, my wife mentioned something of profound importance—consistency.

For the adolescent, socialization takes place on three fronts: 1) the home—the place where God is *modeled*, 2) the church—the place where God is *nurtured*, and 3) the school—the place where God is *taught*. These institutions, when implemented properly, work as one cohesive unit (see diagram A). Each institution should have a positive effect on the developing adolescent. When God is *modeled* in the home, *nurtured* at church, and *taught* at school, there exists adolescent developmental consistency. Keep in mind that each influencing institution filters into the character of the developing adolescent.

God is a constant theme, which increases the godly worldview. As a result, it becomes difficult for the adolescent *not* to make God a part of his decision-making process. God literally becomes a part of the adolescent's construct. It is believed that when one of the influencing institutions fails to present God, there is adolescent developmental dissonance. With adolescent developmental dissonance, the consistency of the God knowledge is removed. However, what we obviously want is developmental consistency. Several years ago I did a study on this very thing. Most of the surveys I collected reflected that most developing Christian adolescents fail to receive God in the school, because the majority of developing Christian adolescents attend public school, where God has been eliminated as a part of the curriculum, barring a few inferences in science or biology.

Each of the three institutions filters information containing lessons of God into the life of the individual from childhood through adolescence, thus creating a Christlike character. It is said that the majority of a personality is a given at birth and nurtured by cultivated habit over an extended period of time, while character formation takes place through an entire life.

Diagram A

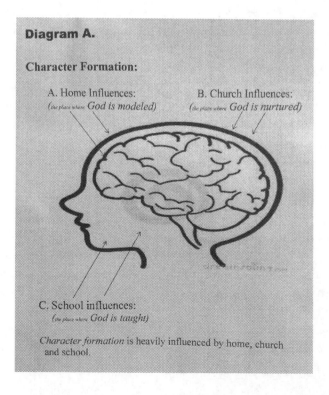

The ideal for the Christian is for teachings of God to permeate the entire life of the individual, giving way to character development for the adolescent.

Diagram B: Adolescent Developmental Consistency

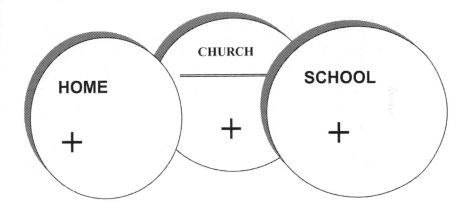

Diagram C: Adolescent Developmental Dissonance

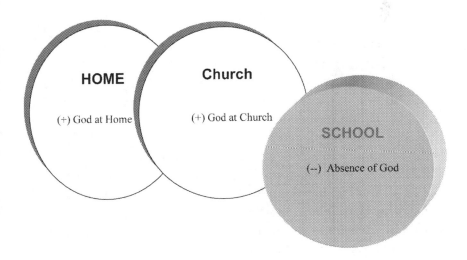

Consistency (Diagram B) exists when the three institutions work as separate but cohesive units. The biblical approach to child and adolescent development is godly exposure from birth through adolescence until the adolescent learns to contract (live on his own) as an adult. Youth are to remain in a consistent environment where God is a constant until they leave home or are able to make mature, principled decisions. This, and only this, is the will of God for His children, decreasing society's negative impressions on the adolescent.

A definition of *dissonance* for my young reader can be defined like it sounds: in disagreement with or incongruent with the other or, in this case, others. Dissonance exists when one of the three institutions disagrees with the others as they try to work together as one cohesive unit. It can be said there are certain times when the opposing unit becomes more of a distraction than the two combined. Although this may not be the norm, it can certainly prove to be disruptive and create dysfunction. For one unit to be in disagreement with the others is not the will of God for His developing adolescent. When such is the case, as it is with most Christian homes across North America where many Christian youth attends public school, the two institutions where God is nurtured and modeled have to compensate for the lack of spirituality in the institution where God is lacking. Again, this is not the will of God for the Christian adolescent.

God in the Home

When growing up, my parents often rehearsed the old adage "actions speak louder than words." Another adage that we all have heard is "a picture is worth a thousand words." One that was favored by my mother was "I'd rather see a sermon than hear a sermon." And a favorite of my father was "I can't hear what you say for what I see what you do."

All these are one in the same. They are simply saying that Christianity is a religion that calls for modeling. Christ was love in action, modeled for all the world to see. Christ modeled the love of God rather than allow it to be passed on by sheer theoretical rhetoric. The home is the place where the love of God is seen in action. Enough cannot be said about modeling Christianity in the home.

Wilmer R. Witte is correct when he writes: "Children are excellent imitators. Much of their education is gained through imitation."[68] As stated, the Christian home is the place where God is modeled. Modeling Christianity is of utmost importance, because children and teens are keen observers. Not only are adolescents observant, but neighbors are quite observant of children's behaviors. It demonstrates how the power of influence is displayed in the community.

The Christian home is that place in the community where object lessons of God are seen daily. We must realize that the power of influence in the home extends far beyond its own members. The majority of society is made up of communities, and communities are made of distinct family units. When God is modeled by parents in the home, these actions spill over in the community by the developing child bringing forth negative or positive behaviors.

Negative Behaviors: "Establish Principles and Set Parameters"

Example 1: Recently, we were visiting family members on vacation. I sat watching a kinetic eighteen-month-old literally manipulate his mother to the point of control. This little fella manifested a certain pattern of behavior in order to get his way; he whined, jerked, pulled, and kicked himself into a sweat until he eventually got the best of his mother, with her soundly giving in. Traveling home, I shared with my wife that the mother had better get a handle on him now, or that trouble would last always—perhaps even beyond adolescence.

Example 2: Sue and Daniel, at the tender age of four, are playing in the bathroom when one unsuspectingly pushes the other. The child lands on the dressing mirror, breaking it. When asked about the incident at the dismissal hour by the teacher and parent, Sue, conveniently forgets. In her own words, when confronted by teacher and parent, she says, "I for-dot."

Yes, she conveniently dismisses the entire incident by stating, "I for-dot." Let's not fool ourselves; negative behaviors are manifest first in the home far in advance of being manifest in the community. As a matter of fact, to repeat scripture of children, "they go astray as soon as they be born speaking lies" (Ps. 58:3). Proverbs 22:15 says, "Foolishness (folly) *is*

---

68   Wilmer R. Witte, "Imitators and Examples," (the Banner, October 3, 1969), 10.

bound in the heart of a child; *but* the rod of correction shall drive it far from him."

Negative behavior literally begins at birth. Therefore, it is critical that principle and parameters are set as early as possible. Obviously, when dealt with at a tender age, issues and problems are easier to tackle than at a later age. As the aging pastor often preached, bend a tree while it is a twig and train a dog when it's a pup, because you can't teach an old dog new tricks. Old dogs are slow to change if they can. That's not saying that an old dog cannot learn new tricks, but the task is increased tenfold when older. The animal's will to learn has diminished over the years. In essence, as time elapses, habits become set and become more difficult to break.

My wife, Ingrid, is a multigrade church school teacher who runs a multigrade school. Ingrid, in my opinion, has mastered teaching the individualized plan for students. This is a plan that develops the full potential of the individual child. We often talk at the end of her lengthy school days about the daily activity and behaviors of her kids. Considering Ingrid's background as a teacher, she is a strong disciplinarian. I use the terminology "her kids" because she interfaces with them literally eight hours of the day.

She tends to take issue with helicopter parents, those who hover over their children and overlook their deficiencies with a sort of false parental guidance and care. When teaching in a Christian, multigrade school, the teacher has the distinct opportunity to monitor the child's behavior and growth process not just daily, but over the years in a guarded environment outside the home. Ingrid has come to realize that when issues surface, some parents—the helicopter parents—have difficulty accepting their children's negative behavior, resulting with the adult subjecting themselves to denial with the statement "not my child."

However, with others, she often hears, "I can believe it. That's Sue." Sometimes, after much discussion, she also has parents who tell her, "Don't worry, Teacher Stanley. We will deal with today's behavior at home." In all honesty, we have to commend those parents who are not in denial, and we pray much for those who are. The worst case scenario is when parents take the child's word over the responsible adult/teacher who literally observes them five days a week.

When negative behaviors are not caught at an early age, the parent is forced to deal with these same behaviors in "teen form" rather than in "child form," which often complicates the matter. This often results in classifying the teen year as the negative period in the child's life. One writer, who I cannot recall, states that when negative behavior occurs before the age of twelve, it's on the parents, but after twelve, it's on the child. What the writer is suggesting is that there is a time in the life of the developing child when parents take the blame; however, after a certain time, the child takes the blame. At this point, the responsibility rests on the developing child. Again, it is critical that principles and parameters are set at an early age.

However, at the stage of adolescence, I can rightfully say that with much patience supplemented with much prayer, the adolescent years can be successful. It is also critical when dealing with latent adolescent issues that parents hold to principles and parameters. When principles and parameters are not set early, it is never too late to start, no matter how difficult the task. When they are not upheld or are violated, you lose your basis for discipline.

Adolescence, as stated before, is often that period when adulthood begins to emerge and the adolescent begins questioning and challenging their learned system of beliefs and values. So, parents, expect a challenge, depending upon the temperament of the adolescent. Remember, there has been a reversal in our righteous nature from a biblical context.

There has also been the myth that adolescence is often the period of negativity. I prefer to use the term *metamorphosis*, or period of change. Metamorphosis suggests a type of change that comes with pain—growing pains that result in something beautiful, which offers hope. I often say that adolescence does not have to be a negative experience. However, when negative behaviors surface, this metamorphosis, or stage of development, requires that same patience supplemented with prayer. You will not have a sense of relief until it is apparent that the adolescent has begun to assume responsibility for her actions. When she takes responsibility for what she does, the principles you have attempted to instill are beginning to take form in her character.

I have *one* son—emphasis on *one*. Coming from a family of eight, I often wondered how parents of yesteryear survived repeat performances of eight children, eight consecutive times, with varying temperaments. Sure, the eldest assisted with younger siblings, but still, having the responsibility of eight can be a tremendous task. Yet, they did it with tremendous success.

I have come to realize there is a type of "common sense-ness" to parenting. Parenting is not as some make it. It is simply applying basic biblical parenting principles. As adults, we must keep in mind that we are not so much trying to be a friend—as I so often hear many today say—as the parent. Too often, in trying to establish relationships with adolescents, some parents sacrifice the parental responsibility factor. Across the board, a friend is treated differently and behaves differently. By the same token, children and teens are treated and behave differently.

Parents have authority over their children and teens and not their friends. Friends come, go, and speak as they please. Children and adolescents are still in the developing stage and oftentimes need guidance and correction. We do a disservice to developing young adults by placing them in settings prematurely (church board/business meetings, etc.) only to occasionally witness a kind of unbecoming adult behavior.

Adding to this, when adolescents are rebellious in school, they are often corrected by adults. When parents have treated them as friends, they expect the same of the public, when such is not the case the majority of the time. Let parents be parents, while at the same time allowing children to be children. However, when Christ is at the center in the home, growth and development is viewed from a higher perspective—a godly, or biblical, perspective.

Love and Kindness

In dealing with young adults, when it comes to negativity and disciplinary issues, the adolescent will eventually respond with willing obedience to the rule of love and kindness. Many use the term "tough love" when it comes to adolescence. With the changing nuclear family and the many single-parent homes, single parents are compelled to pull double-duty, assuming responsibility for both mother and father. The church can be of assistance when parents attend regularly. However, we will deal with the active church later.

Youth have to be commended whenever possible. As my favorite author Ellen Whites states so well, "keep the soil of the heart mellow by the manifestation of love and affection, thus preparing it for the seed of truth—Jesus Christ."[69] Christian child specialists would agree that all children not only need reproof and correction but encouragement and commendation. When this is done from a Christian perspective, heavenly angels stand guard in the home, placing a halo of protection around the family, thus creating a positive influence in the community.

As much as possible, confrontation is to be avoided. White further states, "the wisdom that is of God is first pure, then peaceable, gentle, and easy to be intreated, full of mercy and good fruits, without partiality, and without hypocrisy. And the fruit of righteousness is sown in peace of them that make peace. It is gentleness and peace that Christians are encouraged to strive for in their homes."[70]

Firmness and Kindness

As stated earlier, problems in the home will surface because we live in a morally toxic environment. However, home is the place where trouble should be dealt with in patience, gratitude, and love, while, as one writer states, "keeping sunshine in the heart,"[71] even though the horizon may ever be so cloudy. When Christ's presence is manifest, guardian angels of God will also manifest their presence.

When administering discipline, parents are to be firm and kind. Notice the coupling of words: firmness mingled with kindness—with emphasis on firmness. Without firmness, the adolescent tends to abuse parental kindness. When firmness and kindness are used in tandem early in the life of the child, more often than not, issues are easier to deal with during adolescence. Actually, discipline during the adolescent years is expected.

When these positive graces are modeled before youth, there is the assurance that although families live in a toxic environment morally, we have the promise of scripture that angels of God will stand guard in the home because godly principles are being instituted. The Christian home is that place where illustrations of the true principles of life are displayed, which will be a power for good in the community.

---

[69] Ellen White, *Adventist Home*, 18.

[70] Ibid., 18.

[71] Ibid., 18.

Politeness and Courtesy

When politeness and courtesy is the order of the day in the home, these qualities exert an influence for good. Others in the community will mark the results attained by such a home and will follow the example set, in turn guarding the home against negative influences. It is my personal belief that angels of God often visit the home where the will of God is displayed because the word of God is respected.

When homes are ordered by the known will of God, they become places of delight for those visiting within the confines of their doors. When the will of God is carried out with children, correct habits are formed when there is a careful recognition of the rights of others. A faith that is demonstrated in the home by the love of God purifies the soul, which eventually presides over the entire household and removes any toxic atmosphere.

We should keep in mind that the presence of Christ gives the home peace, making it a place of security. The influence of a carefully guarded Christian home in the years of early childhood and youth is the surest safeguard against a pervasively corrupt society. In the atmosphere of a Christian home, the adolescent will learn to love his parents and God, his Creator. From infancy through adolescence, youth need to have a firm barrier of righteousness built up between them and society, which is a godly home, so that society's corrupting influence may not affect them.

A Case Study: David and Absalom

> And the king was much moved, and went up to the chamber over the gate, and wept: and as he went, thus he said, O my son Absalom, my son, my son Absalom: would God I had died for thee, O Absalom, my son, my son. (2 Sam. 18:33)

In this passage, David is in mourning over his deceased son, Absalom. No parents find joy in having their children precede them in death. However, this is what we discover in 2 Samuel 18—a dysfunctional family in the raw.

It is said that a case study is a record of somebody's problems and how they were dealt with, especially by a psychologist or social worker.

Or it can be an analysis of a particular case or situation used as a basis for drawing conclusions. The Bible itself is actually a case load of real-life stories that we can study and compare to our lives in order to draw sound and wise conclusions. After all, human nature is human nature; from Eden past to Eden restored, human nature will be the same unless dealt with in a spiritual context.

When we read scripture, the Bible does not give man the upper hand. Little is said in regard to humanity. In most cases, the Bible speaks about the human heart as unregenerate and deceitful and above all things desperately wicked (Jer. 17:9).

Let's consider a case study on the life of young Absalom. The name Absalom means "Father of Peace" or "Peace of the Father." When you study his life, you find that his life was one of youthful rebellion in the raw. Contrary to his name, Absalom was not a young man of peace. As a matter of fact, he was a troubled young man, which played itself out though personal vanity and disloyalty to his father due to selfish ambition that caused great strife and open warfare in the royal family. King David, the brilliant and gifted warrior of God, due to his own neglect and domestic problems, suffered one family disaster after another. There are valuable lessons to be learned from Absalom's life.

Lesson 1: "You reap what you sow."

Nothing good proceeds from an evil source. You start with the wrong premise, and you suffer the consequences of your actions. Nathan the Prophet told David that because of his sins of adultery, lying, scheming, and murder, "the sword shall never depart from thine house" (2 Sam. 12:10). Whenever we sin, there are consequences to our actions. David had transgressed the law of God; therefore, because of his egregious act, the life to follow was going to be difficult for the king. Through the experience God caused David to pass through, the Lord shows that He cannot tolerate or excuse sin, whether personal or domestic.

David's history as a parent enables us to see the great ends to which God has in view in His dealings with sin. It enables us to trace the darkest judgments and the working out of God's purposes of mercy, goodness, and beneficence. David was chastised, or to pass under the rod of chastisement, but God did not destroy him. When God uses the furnace, it is to purify, not to consume and destroy. Because of David's sinful acts, God was now in the purification mode for David's salvation and the salvation of his family.

The Bible states: "If they break my statutes, and keep not my commandments; Then will I visit their transgression with the rod, and their iniquity with stripes. Nevertheless my lovingkindness will I not utterly take from him, nor suffer my faithfulness to fail" (Ps. 89:31–33). God will not tolerate or excuse sin in us or our children; we must suffer the consequences of our actions. We reap what we sow.

Where did all the trouble begin with Absalom? The situation with David's numerous wives and concubines created a highly competitive environment for the king and his children. After all, there could only be one successor to the throne, and Absalom wanted it to be him. The trouble actually began when Amnon, David's oldest son, raped his half-sister, Tamar, who was Absalom's full-blooded sister (2 Sam. 13:1–22).

Absalom bided his time, waiting for the right opportunity and the right time to seek revenge on Amnon. Lawfully, Amnon should have been killed. The law pronounced death upon the adulterer, and the unnatural crime of Amnon made him doubly guilty. But David, self-condemned for his own sin, failed to bring Amnon to justice. The shameful crime of Amnon (the firstborn) was permitted by David (the parent) to pass unpunished, unchecked, and unrebuked. Absalom decided in his heart that if his father and king failed to administer justice, he would.

For two full years Absalom, the natural protector of his sister, concealed his purpose of revenge, but only to strike decisively later. Finally, at a feast of the king's sons, the drunken, incestuous Amnon was slain by Absalom's command. Amnon wrongfully assaulted his sister; David, the father and king, failed to correct and rebuke his son; Absalom, in return, committed fratricide against his sibling. This is dysfunction at its worst.

Absalom, knowing what he had done, took refuge with his mother's father at Geshur, where he remained for three years out of reach and out of sight of the king (2 Sam. 13:37–38). When you read the story, you will discover that David loved Absalom. As a matter of fact, you will discover that this kid Absalom was a spoiled brat who, in most cases, got his way. However, because the parent, David, had neglected the duty of punishing the crime of Amnon and because of the unfaithfulness of the king and father and the impenitence of the son, the Lord did not restrain Absalom. Sometimes God permits events to take their natural course.

There is a lesson taught throughout scripture. Ellen G. White states: "When parents or those in authority neglect the duty of correcting wrong, God Himself takes the case in hand." God's restraining power will be, in a measure, removed from the agencies of evil so that a train of circumstances will arise that will correct sin with sin. This is what happened in the case of David and Absalom.

Eventually, David permitted Absalom's return to Jerusalem, but upon his return, more years would pass by before the king agreed to face his son Absalom. Although David mourned Absalom's absence, he still couldn't stand the sight of Absalom because of his deed. This was an act by David that parents fully understand; when adolescents commit deeds that parents disagree with, space and time is needed.

However, while in exile, Absalom made his move to take over the kingdom—not just to merely succeed his father as king but to replace his father while he was still on the throne. Through scheming politics, Absalom managed to gain the support of a large portion of the people and moved to Hebron (the previous capital city of Judah) where he declared himself king while David was king in Jerusalem in the south. With this move, Absalom triggered a civil war between himself and his father. David failed to act with Amnon, and then he failed to act with Absalom (2 Sam. 15:1–12).

The attempted coup was successful; so much so, in fact, that David found it necessary to flee his seat of authority on the throne and run away from Jerusalem to Mahanaim, across the Jordan River. Here is a classic case where the parent loses control of the son. The father is forced to relinquish his seat of authority and power to the recklessness of his son Absalom. Now father and son were put in a position where matters were being settled on the battlefield where Absalom and his followers proved to be no match for the skillful David. Absalom lost twenty thousand of his troops, and the rest were put to flight, proving no match for David's trained men. Not knowing the terrain on the battlefield, while making a hasty retreat in unchartered territory, Absalom caught his head/hair in the branches of an oak tree. While he was still hanging, David's trusted assistant, Joan, drove three javelins through Absalom as he struggled to free himself from the brush and briar. Fallen Prince Absalom died, and his body was thrown into a pit in the forest (2 Sam. 18:1–18). When the battle was over, the question is asked by his father David in concern: "*Is the young man Absalom safe?*" (2 Sam. 18:32).

Absalom was a young man, just learning to contract as an adult with all life's necessities at his fingertips. Absalom had all the makings and components that would warrant success. It is said that in Western society, the recipe for success consists of three ingredients: good looks, money, and intelligence. The Bible says of Absalom, "But in all Israel there was none to be so much praised as Absalom for his beauty: from the sole of his foot even to the crown of his head there was no blemish in him" (2 Sam. 14:25).

Not only was Absalom beautiful, but he was also gifted. When you study the progeny of this young man, you discover that he was a chip off the old block, much like his father David. Remember, the apple does not fall too far from the tree. David himself left a legacy of valiant soldier, military strategist, able administrator, diplomat, composer, and musician—gifted. Genes of intelligence were encoded in the bloodline. Absalom's following consisted of more than twenty thousand soldiers. Needless to say, these people wanted to make Absalom king.

Artfully, Absalom "turned the hearts of the people." Mingling with the people, listening to their grievances, expressing sympathy with their sufferings, and politically highlighting government inefficiency, Absalom won the hearts of the people. Having thus listened to the story of the anonymous man of Israel, prince Absalom replied, "Thy matters are good and right; but there is no man deputed of the king to hear thee," adding, "Oh that I were made judge in the land, that every man which hath *any* suit or cause might come unto me, and I would do him justice" (2 Sam. 15:4). With the minds of the people being prepared for what was to follow, Absalom secretly sent select men throughout the tribes to concert measures for a revolt veiled beneath the cloak of religious devotion with evil designs, which leads to the second lesson.

Lesson 2: Keep it real!

Never use "religion" as a cloak to hide evil motives or intentions. Those who willfully use religious coverings to hide evil or wrong suffer the greatest in the long run. They are best described as hypocrites.

When you read the story carefully, Absalom was beautiful, gifted, energetic, ambitious, unprincipled, impulsive, passionate, and artful, but more so, he was an excellent politician. However, unsanctified beauty and intellect, with added abuse of wealth, creates pride and lends itself to moral collapse.

Lesson 3: Be careful of pride.

Lucifer was called the "son of the morning" and possessed intelligence, beauty, and riches. Lucifer allowed beauty, intellect, and riches to supersede moral fiber. As a result, he lost his moral balance, subsequently falling from glory. Scripture has the following to say about pride:

> The fear of the Lord *is* to hate evil: pride, and arrogancy, and the evil way, and the forward mouth, do I hate. (Prov. 8:13)

> *When* pride cometh, then cometh shame. (Prov. 11:2)

> Price *goeth* before destruction, and a haughty spirit before a fall. (Prov. 16:18)

Lucifer had it all at his fingertips. Both Absalom and Lucifer stumbled from their glorious posts because of pride.

Lesson 4: Surround yourself with good company.

Absalom increasingly received bad counsel from a top official named Ahitophel. Standing next to the king, Ahitophel played a key role encouraging Absalom in incestuous relationships with his father's wives and concubines. It is said that bad company corrupts good morals. Recently, the current youth pop figure, Will.I.Am, was interviewed by a popular TV talk show host. The question was asked, "What would you counsel young people?" His response: "Surround yourself with good friends; get rid of toxic relationships."

The best place for good counsel is the church. In our progressive society, school is mandatory. While some parents may choose to home school their children, on the other hand, for those parents who decide to keep their kids from school for no apparent reason beyond educational purposes, the state has the power to remove the child from the parent for neglect and irresponsibility. In the home, church should not be an option but stated as mandatory.

Lesson 5: Beware of blind affection.

David suffered from mental paralysis of analysis. He could not see the error of his child's ways. Absalom could do no harm and absolutely no wrong in the eyes of his father, the king. King David's own son, the son whom he had loved and trusted, had been planning to seize his crown and to take his life, but he could not see it. Absalom had all the externals, but he was lacking on spiritual internals. This was because of David's own neglect; he allowed his son's negative behavior to go unchecked and uncorrected, which prompted the question, "Is the young man Absalom safe?" David knew Absalom was not safe because of his past behavior and his own personal neglect.

David, with the memory ever before him of his own past transgressions as a parent, seemed morally paralyzed. He was weak and irresolute, when before his personal sin, he had proven to be courageous and decisive. This act of David's neglect should serve as a lesson to parents. There comes a time when, when parents err and others are involved, it would be prudent for parents to confess their mistakes in the presence of their children. David could have corrected his sons by simply admitting where he erred in his decision making and at the same time stating that God had forgiven him. The story of Absalom is a sad but instructive history. The narrative is there as a lesson to be learned in the form of a biblical case study.

God at Church

The Christian believer believes that "enfeebled and defective as it may appear, the church is the one object upon which God bestows in a special sense His supreme regard. It is the theater of His grace, in which He delights to reveal His power to transform hearts.[72] There is a good-natured joke that states there is practically a church on every corner or every other block.

---

[72] Ellen White, *Acts of the Apostles*, 12.

I recently read a poem that gives a negative view to adolescence and the church. It is titled "I Don't."

I Don't
My mother taught me not to smoke, I DON'T,
or listen to a naughty joke, I DON'T.
She told me that I must not wink,
at pretty girls or even think, I DON'T.

Wild youth chase women, wine, and song,
to stay out late is very wrong, I DON'T . . .
I kiss no girls not even one, I don't know how it is done,
you wouldn't think I have much fun, I DON'T!

Author Unknown

The church is the only safe institution we have in society that teaches righteous principles. A community where there is no church has no conscience of morality or positive ethics. To repeat myself, the church is the place where God is nurtured. The second influencing institution that plays an intimate role in shaping the life of the adolescent is the church.

In Matthew 28:18–20, the mission that Christ gave to his disciples was threefold: 1) preach the gospel, 2) baptize and make disciples, and 3) continue teaching the gospel. Christians further believe "when persons who are under conviction are not brought to make a decision at the earliest possible period [in their lives], there is a danger that the conviction [of Christianity] will gradually wear away."[73] Intentional formation of young Christians is the most important ministry contemporary churches can undertake.

Modern liberal education stemming from Rosseau, the eighteenth-century philosopher, assumes that children flourish when given the freedom to select among many options in developing their own unique gifts and talents. This approach can succeed with Christian children, but probably in a culture that is sympathetic with Christian practices and beliefs. Becoming a Christian today is an intentional choice made in the face of other options. While children and adolescents do need freedom, they also need to be deliberately shaped by Christian practices

---

[73] Ellen White, *Evangelism*, 229.

so that they may have a genuine chance to understand and respond to the gospel. Intentional Christian nurturing is necessary, because our culture shapes children for a world that is anti-God.

The church is called upon to rescue people from a world that is antithetical to God and against the dehumanizing currents in popular culture. Children, according to Christian beliefs, are a gift from God. The church stands for a decision to find one's dignity in Jesus Christ. Unless children and adolescents come to know Christ, there is nothing to protect them from hurting themselves and others. There is nothing to help prevent the decay of modern society. Writing during the nineteenth century relative to adolescence and society states:

> The evil influence around our children is almost overpowering; it is corrupting their minds and leading them down to perdition. The minds of youth are naturally given to folly; and at an early age, before their characters are formed, and their judgment matured, they frequently manifest a preference for associates who will have an injurious influence over them. Some form attachments for the other sex, contrary to the wishes and entreaties of their parents, and break the fifth commandment by thus dishonoring them. It is the duty of parents to watch the going out and the coming in of their children.[74]

If the above statement was penned in the nineteenth century, what could be said of society's influences in the twenty-first century?

The church is perhaps the only institution with the beliefs, liturgy, practices, social structure, and authority—enfeebled though it be—necessary to rescue children and adolescents from the violence and other deforming features of twenty-first-century life. As King David believes, this can neither be accomplished by simply laying the faith before adolescents and inviting them to choose it nor by imposing Christian identity through force and indoctrination. The church can help prepare the setting for the Holy Spirit's influences, slowly nurturing children and adolescents into the Christian faith and practice. According to Ellen

---

[74] Ellen White, *Testimonies for the Church*, 165.

Charry, churches need to think creatively about how to assist the Spirit's influence in this process of shaping.[75]

The church is best positioned to form Christian character, along with the Christian home and school for character development. The church is one of the few institutions with access to the entire family. Both parents and children are brought into the church's sphere intellectually, spiritually, and socially where they can publicly interact with one another and find support for their life as a family. In addition to this, the pulpit offers perhaps the remaining locus of personal and public edification and exhortation. The church is one institution that is interested in the adolescent's moral, social, and intellectual development.

Charry states that even skilled parents cannot raise children alone; the authority of popular culture is too strong. Adolescents need the support and advice of the church. The church also creates an environment where there exists a variety of people—both other children and young adults, friends and strangers—in order to develop a proper range of social skills. Placing teens in selective environments can help mold and fashion them. Children and adolescents, according to Charry, need to see themselves as a part of a community larger than their immediate families and to have their growing knowledge and love of God nurtured by people other than their parents. This is especially true of adolescents, as teens explore the world beyond family and the authority of the peer group and the general culture increases.

The church also sets the tone for adolescents by the programs it offers. Each church must make the commitment to programs that would cater to the spiritual growth of their youth. Netterburg and Wheeler state that "a church that includes youth in its world is a church that youth include in theirs."[76] A church that wants its youth to grow in their faith and remain committed church members as adults must first demonstrate commitment to it adolescents.

Two studies conducted by a popular denomination titled Valuegenesis Studies I and II, along with my personal research, tell us that churches must have two important qualities to grow strong youth: they must be warm and caring, and they must encourage honesty and spiritual independent

---

75   Karen Yust, *Nurturing Child and Adolescent Spirituality,* 20.
76   K. Netteburg and T. Wheeler, *Every Child Should Be Church-Schooled,* 35–37.

thinking. Steve Case, youth program director, notes that one of the most important facets of helping children be close to the church is for them to have caring peers. "Youth need to experience support and concern from peers in church frequently,"[77] he notes. Case recommends that adults need to set the tone to provide a friendly atmosphere that encourages discussion, questioning, and independent thinking. This can be done by the tone of the programs it offers. This goes back to the Holden theory of "think, young people think!"

God in the School

Ellen White states, "Higher than the highest human thought can reach is God's ideal for His children." It is indeed a keen observation that outside of the home, the school is the second institution where adolescents spend the majority of their time—in the classroom where God is not taught. The school is one of the areas where kids are most vulnerable. Friendships are formed, and influences are strong. Quite literally, students and teachers live a large share of their lives together. Because they share this time, it is important that the teacher has a biblical foundation. They are not only teachers and pupils in the narrower sense, but they are Christian human beings handling life's problems in each other's presence five days a week. With seven to eight hours of each day in each other's presence, it can almost be said that students live with their teachers in more subtle ways than can be realized. Here is where a Christian teacher is vital. The student learns by means of observation (Mark 3:14). Not only is the student learning theory, but he is also learning application and correlating the two.

Jesus, quite frankly, illustrated this all the time. In Acts 4:13, the followers of Jesus imitated the life of Christ so well that their enemies took note of the fact that the knowledge and behavior of the disciples clearly indicated that they had been "with Jesus," their master. Jesus was oftentimes referred to as teacher or master. When the term master was used in the New Testament setting, it was often used in a teacher/student milieu.

---

[77] Steve Case, *"Valuegenesis: Is Anyone Listening?" Adventist Today* (Nov./Dec. 1993): 31-32.

Having grown up in a denomination where a premium is placed on education, I believe too much emphasis has been placed on the teacher. What should have been done in the home the teacher is oftentimes left to correct. This is not what God intended. Christian modeling should take place in the home environment, and theory is to be presented in the classroom.

The teacher has been brought together with his pupils for a purpose much larger than lecture; both teacher and pupil need each other for life. Each furnishes much of the necessary content of the other's life during the hours and time spent with each other. Relationships exist, grow, change, develop, and, from time to time, break down.

As stated earlier, my wife is a teacher. She has encountered students who when they were small, and I quote, "hated her guts." But as they spent time together, the relationship subtly changed for the better over time. Christian education, at its heart, is first character building. We must not fail to forget that our ultimate home is paradise. When educated for God, the mind carries with it at best long-term values that stretch into eternity. Earthly values at their best are short-term. I would like to end this section with a statement from a father who suffered the loss of a child in one of America's worst tragedies—the 1999 school shooting in Columbine, Colorado.

"Since the dawn of creation there has been both good and evil in the hearts of men and women. We all contain the seeds of kindness or the seeds of violence. The death of my wonderful daughter, Rachel Joy Scott, and the deaths of that heroic teacher, and the other eleven children who died, must not be in vain. Their blood cries out for answers.

"The first recorded act of violence was when Cain slew his brother Abel out in the field. The villain was not the club he used. Neither was it the NCA (National Club Association). The true killer was Cain, and the reason for the murder could only be found in Cain's heart.

"In the days that followed the Columbine tragedy, I was amazed at how quickly fingers began to be pointed at groups such as the NRA. I am not a member of the NRA. I am not a hunter. I do not even own a gun. I am not here to represent or defend the NRA—because I don't believe that they are responsible for my daughter's death. Therefore I do not believe that they need to be defended. If I believed they had anything to do with Rachel's murder I would be their strongest opponent.

"I am here today to declare that Columbine was not just a tragedy—it was a spiritual event that should be forcing us to look at where the real blame lies! Much of the blame lies here in this room. Much of the blame lies behind the pointing fingers of the accusers themselves. I wrote a poem just four nights ago that expresses my feelings best."

> Your laws ignore our deepest needs,
> Your words are empty air.
> You've stripped away our heritage,
> You've outlawed simple prayer.
> Now gunshots fill our classrooms,
> and precious children die.
> You seek for answers everywhere,
> and ask the question "Why?"
> You regulate restrictive laws,
> Through legislative creed.
> And yet you fail to understand,
> that God is what we need!

"Men and women are three-part beings. We all consist of body, mind, and spirit. When we refuse to acknowledge a third part of our makeup, we create a void that allows evil, prejudice, and hatred to rush in and wreak havoc. Spiritual presences were present within our educational systems for most of our nation's history. Many of our major colleges began as theological seminaries. This is a historical fact. What has happened to us as a nation? We have refused to honor God, and in so doing, we open the doors to hatred and violence. And when something as terrible as Columbine's tragedy occurs—politicians immediately look for a scapegoat such as the NRA. They immediately seek to pass more restrictive laws that contribute to erode away our personal and private liberties. We do not need more restrictive laws. Eric and Dylan would not have been stopped by metal detectors. No amount of gun laws can stop someone who spends months planning this type of massacre. The real villain lies within our own hearts.

"As my son Craig lay under that table in the school library and saw his two friends murdered before his very eyes, he did not hesitate to pray in school. I defy any law or politician to deny him that right! I challenge every young person in America, and around the world, to realize that on

April 20, 1999, at Columbine High School prayer was brought back to our schools. Do not let the many prayers offered by those students be in vain. Dare to move into the new millennium with a sacred disregard for legislation that violates your God-given right to communicate with Him. To those of you who would point your finger at the NRA—I give to you a sincere challenge. Dare to examine your own heart before casting the first stone! My daughter's death will not be in vain! The young people of this country will not allow that to happen!"

PART II

COUNSELING THE ADOLESCENT

CHAPTER SEVEN

RELATIONSHIPS! Relationships!

RELATIONSHIPS!

One year ago, I returned to speak at one of my previous churches for its fiftieth anniversary. Much of the reminiscing involved the relationships I had developed with the youth. Counseling today's adolescents, believe it or not, I have come to accept that it's all about relationships—relationships you have developed over a short or extended period of time. Very seldom will youth vent their "issues of the heart" to any authority figure unless they feel a certain level of comfort.

As a pastor, I spent a lot of time—fifteen-plus years—at summer camp on the lakefront steering boats and Jet Skis, with ropes and skis attached, teaching youth the sports. As I reflect on those hot and sometimes humid Texas summers, beyond watching adolescents fall face-first into the lake and tumble across the surface with detached skis going one way and body another, what I enjoyed most was lazily sitting in the boat or under the shade tree. That's where I would socialize with the youth as I kicked back to relax with my feet bare, my legs crossed, and my cap pulled nearly over my eyes. What I discovered by summer's end was that quite a number of adolescents who attended camp became open and transparent in their relationships with caring workers.

Transparency became the method by which we began to view each other. Both the adolescent and I began to see each other in our humanness, which contributed to meaningful and lasting relationships. Because I am very much into sports (snowboarding, snow and water skiing, scuba diving, cycling, running, hiking, sailing), I oftentimes invite the many adolescents I have come to know as a pastor over the years into my world of activity in an attempt to foster and encourage positive Christian relationships. Vacation Bible school, youth Bible class, youth society gatherings, meetings, and many other church programs were vehicles we used to develop youthful social relations. As an interested and sincere pastor, it was difficult for my youth not to have some sort of social contact with me. As a matter of fact, I planned it that way.

Currently, I pastor a multichurch district. As stated earlier, my wife is the principal/teacher at a small church school. Through her work, I continue to develop relationships with her/my kids by taking an active part in their academic and social events. From time to time, I—to my wife's dismay—walk disruptively through her class comically pulling hair, snatching caps and backpacks, plucking earlobes, and distracting youth. I also take the time to referee soccer and baseball games—all in an attempt to develop relationships. What I have come to enjoy most are fist bumps. When they do well, they rush to the pastor to receive a pastoral fist bump. Relationships! By the way, pastors and leaders, when you leave that district, you have left an impression that is very difficult to erase. You have made definite impressions on developing minds.

Years before pastoring, while I was still in college, I took a hiatus to the country of Japan as a student missionary teaching conversational English. Lasting relationships were developed not so much in the classroom where I spent countless hours drilling students, but instead outside of class on the social front where I interacted and mingled in gatherings with family members. Why state this? It is my firm belief that counseling and understanding the adolescent is all about relationships. Relationships that develop over a period of time—whether short or long—leave lasting impressions on the developing adolescent, hopefully for the better.

At the center of all Christian counseling is Jesus Christ. When counseling, it is vital that the counselor remain Christ-centered. Too often, the counselee tends to become dependent on the counselor, creating long-term situations rather than short-term, creating codependency.[78]

---

[78] There will be times (in my opinion), when long-term counseling situations may be needed, depending on the issue(s). It is not always wise to create long-term situations. Most counseling sessions should not be more than twelve sessions. The objective of every Christian and adolescent counselor should be to encourage independency. If there is codependency, make sure Christ is in tandem with the counselee and not the counselor. The majority of Christ counseling situations were short-term situations with a long-term effect and not the other way around. Another matter that deserves attentions is knowing when to draw the line, cut off, or refer.

Counselors want to make the counselee dependent on the Savior for lasting situations. Christ always pointed those with whom he came in contact with to the Father. There is a need for the counselor to pray often when listening to individuals, such that the counselee and counselor can learn to trust in God for solutions to their problems as Jesus often encouraged.

For well over twenty-five years, I have listened to people and their problems, and I can conclude that whenever there is a problem, there is always a solution. I may not have the answer to the problem, because my timing may not always be on cue, but pointing the counselee to Christ takes away the codependency status. When the counselor can rightfully point the counselee to God, the counselee is now learning to develop a relationship.

When you think about it, the Bible is a book that is built on relationships—social relationships. From the inception of the creation of man, God has sought to effectively communicate and build relationships with His children. Christ was nothing more than an itinerant Messiah, constantly on the move. Quite often, there were times when Christ would take Palestinian siestas, reclining and socializing in the homes of converts while relishing home-cooked meals. As a result, He was constantly accused of bad associations. But He established these relationships in order to save.

Such was the case in Bethany, the home of Lazarus and Martha, where Mary comfortably sat at Jesus's feet (Luke 10:39). I picture Jesus as one who was motivated by a mission of saving and building lasting relationships. Christ spent thirty-three and a half years on Earth, with three and a half of those years socially engaged with twelve disciples and others from different backgrounds and various walks of life, He gave them a piece of himself through mentoring principles to live by.

If we want to have a part in reaching youth, we must sacrifice time mentoring through biblical principles and building relationship in an attempt to propel the adolescent toward Christ. It has been stated that in order to build a relationship with Jesus as Christians, "we must spend a thoughtful hour, each day, in contemplation of the life of Christ."[79] You may want to start with thirty minutes. With adolescents, the principle is the same. We must put in the time if we are to build lasting relationships with adolescents instilling eternal values.

---

[79] Ellen White, *Desire of Ages*, 83.

Adolescents are real people with real questions who are seeking real answers. After all, adolescents' transitional years are considered to be a period of searching for answers to life's issues and their place in society. There are two objectives to keep in mind when counseling the adolescent: First, bring the adolescent to a saving knowledge of Christ as Savior and Lord, turning attention away from himself and others to Christ. Second, we must help the adolescent to understand that Christ has become a lifetime counselor, companion, and friend who has his best interest at heart, someone to depend on in times of crisis and tranquility. Once these major objectives are realized, daily challenges will become less demanding, and everyday life will be more fulfilling for both the counselor and counselee.

Issues of the Heart

Because Jesus was God in the flesh, counseling became relatively easy for the master. Jesus could read the thoughts and motives of individuals, which often allowed Him to cut to the chase and get to the issues of the heart. Christ knew the content matter that existed in the hearts of all humanity. Christian counselors, on the other hand, who are unlike Christ, cannot see what actually takes place in the human heart. Therefore, it may take us longer to figure out what actually makes a person tick or what it is that she treasures most. So how do we come by our data? By listening and reading the actions of the individual.

The question that remains is how do we come to understand what goes on in the heart of a person? Here is what Jeremiah says about the heart: "the heart *is* deceitful above all *things*, and desperately wicked: who can know it?" (Jer. 17:9). Since the fall of humanity, the heart has been naturally deceptive. It naturally operates in opposition to the design of God. However, in Jeremiah 17:10, the prophet follows up with the answer to his own question: "I know mans heart. I know how his minds works. I examine his heart and test his thinking. I reward him for what he has done, according to the fruit of his life." Though humans are prone to self-deception, which leads away from the Lord, and it is impossible for them to see the danger of self-deception, God knows exactly what goes on in the heart of every person.

In Proverbs 21:2, it says, "Every way of a man *is* right in his own eyes: but the Lord pondereth the hearts." In Solomon's prayer of consecration after the temple's construction, Solomon entreated the Lord to hear the prayers of his people if they ever become afflicted. If they ever lifted their hands toward his house, he asked this request of the Lord: "Then hear thou *in* heaven thy dwelling place, and forgive, and do, and give to every man according to his ways, whose heart thou knowest; (for thou, *even* thou only, knowest the hearts of all the children of men)" (1 Kings 8:39).

Counseling is really an attempt to get to the issues in the heart. When we think of the heart, we think of the physical organ that pumps blood through arteries and veins and the various parts of the body. However, in the scriptures, the heart is viewed quite differently. Proverbs 4:20–23 says:

"My son, attend to my words; incline thine ear unto my sayings. Let them not depart from thine eyes; keep them in the midst of thine heart. For they *are* life unto those that find them, and health to all their flesh. Keep thy heart with all diligence; for out of it [are] the issues of life.

This passage seems to suggest that a father implores his son to take his counsel seriously. In emphasizing this point, the father makes two observations using the word heart. In verse 21, the father encourages his son to keep his words or sayings within his heart. In verse 23, the father says, "keep your heart with all vigilance." The New International Version states, "above all else guard the heart." These verses appear to suggest that the heart is a place of emotions.

Verse 23 says, "for from it flows the spring of life." Lifestyle choices flow out of the heart. The Hebrew writing in verse 23 reads more literally "from it, the goings out of life." Regarding this Hebrew word *heart*, Roland Murphy writes:

> It is often paraphrased as mind since it does have an intellectual component. It is also the basic orientation of a person embracing desires, emotions, and attitudes. Whatever fills the heart, whatever is within the heart of a person comes out of the heart in terms of that person's behavior speech and attitude. As in water, face reflects face, so the heart of man reflects the man.

Jesus also uses the word *heart* in a similar way as do the wisdom writers in the Old Testament. In Matthew 6, Jesus teaches us about the hearts role in motivation:

> Lay not up for yourselves treasures upon earth, where moth and rust doth corrupt, and where thieves break through and steal: But lay up for yourselves treasures in heaven, where neither moth nor rust doth corrupt, and where thieves do not break through nor steal: For where your treasure is, there will your heart be also. (Matt. 6:19–21)

These passages seem to suggest that whatever a person values the most will be evident in that person's behavior. If a person desires earthly possessions, then that person's lifestyle will reflect that passion. If a person values spiritual treasure, then that person's lifestyle will reflect that passion. Thus, Jesus's way of thinking is that motivation is a matter of what a person treasures in his heart. If you want to understand why people do what they do, you might ask, "What is it that they treasure most?"

On another occasion, Jesus was confronting His disciples on their slowness to comprehend His teachings. No one is really unclean because they do not partake of ceremonial washings or because of eating certain foods (Mark 7:3–8). It's not what goes into the temple that renders them unclean, Christ points out; instead, it's what comes out of a man.

Among the things that Christ lists in Mark 7:21–22 are thoughts, behaviors, and desires. In other words, the heart is the source of motivation, direction, and morality for lifestyle choices. Matthew states both the bad and the good are said to have their roots in the heart. The heart is defined rather as the center, or source, of direction, motivation, and morality for lifestyle choices, and in turn, those lifestyle choices are going to be represented in a person's behavior patterns, thinking patterns, and feeling patterns.

Case Study: Cain and Abel

In Genesis 4:1–16, we find the story of Cain and Abel:

> And Adam knew Eve his wife; and she conceived, and bare Cain, and said, I have gotten a man from the Lord. And she again bare his brother Abel. And Abel was a keeper of sheep, but Cain was a tiller of the ground. And in process of time it came to pass, that Cain brought of the fruit of the ground

an offering unto the Lord. And Abel, he also brought of the firstlings of his flock and of the fat thereof. And the Lord had respect unto Abel and to his offering: But unto Cain and to his offering he had not respect. And Cain was very wroth, and his countenance fell. And the Lord said unto Cain, Why art thou wroth? and why is thy countenance fallen? If thou doest well, *shalt thou* not be accepted? and if thou doest not well, sin lieth at the door. And unto thee *shall be* his desire, and thou shalt rule over him. And Cain talked with Abel his brother: and it came to pass, when they were in the field, that Cain rose up against Abel his brother, and slew him. And the Lord said unto Cain, Where *is* Abel thy brother? And he said, I know now: *Am I my brother's keeper?* And he said, What hast thou done? the voice of thy brother's blood crieth unto me from the ground. And now *art* thou cursed from the earth, which hath opened her mouth to receive thy brother's blood from thy hand. When thou tillest the ground, it shall not henceforth yield unto thee her strength; a fugitive and a vagabond shalt thou be in the earth. And Cain said unto the Lord, My punishment is greater than I can bear. Behold, thou hast driven me out *this* day from the face of the earth; and from thy face shall I be hid; and I shall be a fugitive and a vagabond in the earth; and it shall come to pass, *that* every one that findeth me shall slay me. And the Lord said unto him, Therefore whosoever slayeth Cain, vengeance shall be taken on him sevenfold. And the Lord set a mark upon Cain, lest any finding him should kill him. And Cain went out from the presence of the Lord, and dwelt in the land of Nod, on the east of Eden.

This incident takes place after the introduction of sin (Gen. 3). It is one of excitement and anticipation after the devastating tree incident. Eve, with exclamation, looks forward to their firstborn child. She says, in essence, as stated in the Clear Word Paraphrase: "I have given birth to a man!" Eve had high hopes that this male child was the promised redeemer.[80] However, here is the case in the world's first family where

---

[80] Genesis 3:15, Blanco, Jack. The Clear Word Paraphrase

things go from the sublime to the ridiculous and from the ridiculous to the disastrous.

They have just suffered the loss of paradise, and now they suffer the loss of their second born at the hands of their firstborn. This incident is not just another story to be rehearsed, but it is a real-to-life human drama taking place within the confines of the first family. Catch the scene: Abel is lying motionless on the ground. His lungs are now empty, no more breath in the cavity of his chest. His heart has stopped, and he will not be getting up. Beneath him, the innocent flowers shudder from the weight of spilled blood; above him, his guilty brother shivers, the murder weapon still dripping blood in his hand. Beyond them both, a holy God looks down with grief to see and witness what has become of His creation. The great controversy that had begun in heaven between Christ and Satan has escalated to engulf planet Earth, and Abel has now become the very first human casualty.

We are spared the details and are not told how Cain performed his dastardly deed. The Bible suggests that the act of murder is enough—why go into the gory details of the act itself? We only know that the world's first baby has become the world's first murderer, and neither he nor the world will ever be the same again. Cain does not know it, but his sin has set off a chain of violence that has circled the globe from that day forward. Satan has used murder as one of his special tools to ruin human souls—both the soul of victim and perpetrator. And before he is finished, not only will brother be killing brother, but husbands wives, and wives husbands, children their parents, and nation in a holocaust of bloodshed that will plague the human family till the end of time.

To this day, from that one incident, we have a new vocabulary of terminology—words to describe killings like homicide, fratricide, infanticide, feticide, genocide, and suicide; words like massacre, manslaughter, assassination, and annihilation. We all have those words now. We all know what they mean, but the thought never entered the mind of Cain.

By the time this story reaches the New Testament, the emphasis is clearly on motivation. It is not Abel's deeds or the wound that is discussed in 1 John 3 or how many blows were struck or what weapon was used, as if we are dealing with legalities. By the time the story is taken up in the New Testament, the focus is on motivation behind the behavior. What are the issues in the heart that controls Cain? What was it that motivated the elder to kill the younger? "The heart *is* deceitful above all *things*, and desperately wicked: who can know it?" (Jer. 17:9–10). It was a case of one who was evil slaying the one who was righteous. In the New Testament,[81] Jesus spoke of the righteous blood of Abel crying from the earth. 1 John 3:12 suggested Abel's works were righteous, while Cain's works were evil. In this incident, two natures begin to emerge relationally; the righteous nature of Abel and the evil nature of Cain. One child's nature bends toward righteousness, and the other's bends toward evil. Today Cain would be labeled the black sheep of the family or the negative, and there are those who tend toward righteousness or the good.

The meanings of their names give us glimpses into their characters. Abel means "breath" or "life." Cain, on the other hand, means "possessed." Cain was possessed with the spirit of the evil one. They emerge not as twins, look-alikes, or Siamese twins, but rather opposites. And when opposites emerge, there is conflict soon to follow—and disagreements, variance, and quarrels, as well as diverging opinions, beliefs, and philosophies. What began to emerge in their association with each other are issues of the heart.

Cain and Abel differed widely in character. Abel had a spirit of loyalty to God, seeing the justice and mercy of God in dealings with the fallen race. He accepted the hope of redemption—the redeeming blood of Jesus, through his daily sacrifice which pointed to the death of Christ on the cross. But Cain, on the other hand, cherished feelings of rebellion, always murmuring against God and blaming God for the curse pronounced upon the earth and upon the human race for Adam's sin.

Cain permitted his mind to run in the same channel that led to Satan's fall—indulging the desire for self-exaltation and questioning the justice and authority of God, thus causing himself to run amuck spiritually, socially, mentally, and physically. Adam, Eve, Cain, and Abel had been told to bring a lamb when they came to the altar; this represented the blood of Jesus. Adam, Eve, and Abel came to the altar with the appropriate sacrifice. Cain, on the other hand, when coming to the altar, brought his crops; because he had no lamb, his sacrifice lacked the blood.

Cain chose not to do it the way God wanted it to be done. Instead, he chose to fulfill the demands of God the way he saw fit. We fail from time to time as believers in Christ to realize that God means what he says.

---

[81]   Matthew 23:35.

When Naaman was instructed to go and dip seven times in the muddy Jordan, God did not want Naaman to go and dip in the clean waters of the Pharphar River (2 Kings 5:12). When God demanded that only the priest touch the Ark of the Covenant, anyone outside of the specifics of God meant danger. So when Uzzah touched the Ark containing the commandments of God, he died (1 Chron. 13:9–10). Substitutes in place of the specifics of God prove fatal in the long haul. Cain's mistakes prove fatal.

Abel brought his offering in faith, while Cain's offering was without faith. Abel came with the Spirit of Christ, while Cain was "possessed" with the spirit of the evil one. Abel's offering was accepted, while Cain's offering was rejected. Abel served God in a righteous way, while Cain served God in a selfish way. Issues of the heart were at stake.

As brothers often do today, secluded back in their bedroom, picture Abel pleading with his sibling to approach God in the divinely prescribed manner to avoid the retributive judgment of God. Cain chose to come before God with his own merits when he should have come in the merits of Christ—the sacrificial lamb. When Abel brought his offering, fire leaped from glory and consumed his offering. There was no fire from glory to consume the offering of Cain.

Murder, as we have come to know it, does not just happen. It begins with a thought, which is later conceptualized and carried out or planned by design in our actions. Cain had thoughts of evil. Parents who are in-touch with their children are aware of their children's problems and issues. Adam and Eve probably struggled with getting Cain to come to worship. Grudgingly, Cain is descriptive of a young man whom parents dragged to church whining, complaining, and kicking, making family life miserable.

Thoughts that consume the heart are eventually played out in the actions. Cain strikes his younger brother, fatally killing him. Causative studies of the life of Cain would conclude with a profile of negative family history. Some would conclude, while I may tend to disagree, that religion was overplayed in the home, which proved fatal. Social scientists would conclude from Cain's actions that he was an angry child with thoughts of hate toward God and his fellow man. He did not look upon God as a God of mercy, but instead questioned the acts of God—negative, unchecked thoughts that are harbored in the mind always prove detrimental. Cain harbored negative thoughts against God, his family, and his brother in his heart that eventually played out in life.

What does the Bible say about the heart? "Out of the abundance of the heart the mouth speaketh" (Matt. 12:34). My mother, who was an old farm girl from Louisiana, always had this saying, "The cream will always rise to the top." Translated in laymen terms, what you think will always eventually surface as truth in action. If evil is nesting in the heart, evil will surface. Likewise, if truth is hidden in the heart, it too will surface in actions. As the old adage goes, a picture is worth a thousand words. With Cain, he brought what he wanted to bring to God.

God finally confronts Cain in Genesis 4:7: "If thou doest well, *shalt thou* not be accepted? And if thou doest not well, sin lieth at the door. And unto thee *shall be* his desire, and thou shalt rule over him." God read Cain's heart, knowing there were hidden issues of sin in the heart, knowing that if Cain chose not to obey righteously, those hidden issues would later surface in a more destructive form. Notice God's wording (I am paraphrasing here.): "If you do not take care of the hidden sin in the heart, it's waiting as a hidden robber to overpower you." God personifies sin in Genesis 4:7 by giving sin legs and a body, describes it as playing the role of a robber or criminal, lurking to destroy.

Not only did Cain show it in his offerings what he was thinking in his heart, but he showed it in his countenance. His countenance had fallen. In fact, God asks him, "Why is thy countenance fallen?" (Gen. 4:6). The Clear Word paraphrase states, "Why is your face so distorted?" Cain did not have a happy face. The heart's issues were beginning to seep through and burn into his countenance until it came out in the fatal act of murder. When approached, Cain becomes sarcastically evasive, "Am I my brother's keeper?" (Gen. 4:9) he asks, attempting to display a type of nonchalance that suggests brotherly indifference. While there was still time to confess and repent, remorse had taken hold in his heart.

According to the law, Cain should have been killed. He had taken the life of someone by the act of sin, and the wages of sin is death. God selectively chose to banish Cain instead of killing him. In sparing his life, God gave the world an example of what would be the result of permitting the sinner to live to continue a course of unbridled iniquity. Through the influence of Cain's teaching and example, many of his descendants would be led into sin until, when prior to the flood, "the wickedness of man *was* great in the earth," and "every imagination of the thoughts of his heart *was* only evil continually" (Gen. 6:5). This forced the hand of God to destroy the earth in a flood. Cain went out from the presence of the Lord to seek his home; just as the prodigal wandered into the far country, so do sinners seek happiness in forgetfulness of God. The case of Cain and Abel is a study of what happens when sin is not confronted in the heart.

Nouthetic Counseling

Before I can give you an approach to counseling, you must understand nouthetic counseling. This approach to counseling was made famous by Dr. Jay Adams and is still unknown by many. Nouthetic counseling is basically a big phrase for "confronting the issues with truth" and going straight to the heart of the matter.

The term *nouthetic* comes from the Greek words *nouthesis* and *noutheteo*, which are noun and verb forms used in the New Testament meaning "to confront." In Colossians 3:16, Paul urged, "Let the word of Christ dwell in you richly in all wisdom; teaching and admonishing one another [confronting one another] in psalms and hymns and spiritual songs, singing with grace in your hearts to the Lord." According to Paul, all Christians must teach and confront one another in a nouthetic way. In support of this, Paul also wrote in Romans 15:14, "And I myself also am persuaded of you, my brethren, that ye also are full of goodness, filled with all knowledge, able also to admonish one another[to confront one another nouthetically]."

Unlike many counselors today, Jesus's counseling was more short-term than long-term. When dealing with lost humanity, Christ was always patient but nouthetically straight to the point. Seldom do you read where there was a recurrence of Jesus dealing with a case study more than once. Once introduced to the saving knowledge of the Master, there was a continuum and a building on that initial experience. *Sanctification* is the adopted theological term we use to describe the process of developing a daily walk and relationship with Christ for a lifetime.

Nouthetic confrontation, according to Jay Adams, consists of at least three basic elements: 1) problems, 2) solutions, and 3) motive. Let's consider each.

Nouthetic confrontation always implies a problem and presupposes an obstacle that must be overcome; something is wrong in the life of the one who is confronted. Jay Adams says that some degree of opposition has been encountered, and one wishes to subdue or remove it, not by punishment but by influencing the mind.[82] Nouthesis specifically presupposes the need for a change in the person confronted who may or may not put up some resistance. However, it is obvious that nouthetic confrontation suggests that there is something wrong with the person who is to be confronted. There is some wrong, some sin, in the individual's life—an obstruction, problem, difficulty, or need that has to be acknowledged and dealt with. The fundamental purpose of nouthetic confrontation is to effect personality and behavioral change.

The second element in the concept of nouthetic confrontation is that problems are solved nouthetically by verbal means—words of encouragement, remonstrance, reproof, and words of blame where they may be required. There is person-to-person verbal confrontation. Nouthesis presupposes a counseling type of confrontation in which the object is to cause a character and behavioral change in the adolescent or counselee.

Some biblical examples of such confrontations are Nathan confronting David after his sin with Uriah and Bathsheba and Christ restoring Peter after His resurrection. The failure to confront nouthetically may be seen in the blameworthy behavior of Eli recorded in 1 Samuel 3:13: "I told him I would no longer uphold his family in the priesthood because the behavior of his sons has brought contempt on the ministry and destroyed the people's respect for their God. Eli knew what his sons were doing and did nothing about it, nor did he put them out of the ministry." Eli's sin was failure to confront his sons nouthetically.

Failing to speak or confront them seriously enough to cause genuine change in them proved to be fatal. He failed to correct them a little too late. When you read the incident in I Samuel 2:23-24, Eli said, "Why do you keep doing such wicked things? Over the years I've heard about all what you've been doing, but I kept praying that you would come to your senses. What I hear is not good. Everywhere I go the Lord's people are talking about you." He describes his sons' behavior as "misconduct," which were literally sinful things. Eli failed to qualify their actions as sinful. It was Eli's task to stop them, but he failed to take action.

With most counseling sessions, there is the task of gathering historical data or long incursions back into the intricacies of the whys and wherefores

---

[82]   Jay Adams, *Competent to Counsel*, 120.

of behavior. However, with nouthetic counseling, the emphasis is placed on the *what*. What was done? What must be done to rectify it? And what should the future response be? The *why* is established already because of the nature of the sinful heart. We are born sinners. The *what* tends to lead to solutions to the problem, whereas the *why* tends toward blame shifting. Nouthetic counseling seeks to correct sinful behavior patterns by personal confrontation with confession and repentance.

The third element in the word *nouthesis* has in view the motive behind the confronted and questionable activity. With nouthetic counseling, the verbal correction is intended to benefit the adolescent. The goal must be to meet obstacles head on and overcome them verbally, not in order to punish but instead to help and assist the adolescent toward better and godlier behavior. According to Jay Adams, whom I consider to be the father of the nouthetic counseling, nouthesis is motivated by love and deep concern for the youth, in which the adolescents are counseled and corrected by verbal means for their good, ultimately for the glorification of God.

With nouthetic counseling, scripture plays an intimate role in the process. In 2 Timothy 3:16–17, it says, "All scripture *is* given by inspiration of God, and *is* profitable for doctrine, for reproof, for correction, for instruction in righteousness: That the man of God may be perfect, thoroughly furnished unto all good works." The scriptures are nouthetically oriented in that they are written for correction, reproof, and instruction in righteousness, perfecting the man of God and training him in righteousness.

The scriptures are inspired, meaning God-breathed, the very spoken words of God. So nouthetic confrontation should instead be scriptural confrontation. What is passed on to the counselee from the counselor should be taken from the word of God, eclipsing the counsel of man for the counsel of God. Nouthetic counseling removes man off the hot seat and places God there instead, thus allowing God to take precedence over human wisdom. This also removes cause for blame shifting and criticism for the counselor. Nouthetic confrontation is, in short, confrontation with the principles and practices of the scriptures. You are confronting with the word of God.

The Apostle Paul had a knack for becoming involved with his people. In Acts 20, Paul talks about pastoring "with tears." Paul became an involved personality. Youth counselors must become involved with the youth whom they are counseling. I have noticed over the years that youth can quickly pick up insincerity. As a serious college student, I vividly recall several college presidents during my tenure as a student. After a semester of watching the president's involvement and interfacing with the student body, the students could tell if he was truly sincere.

Youth can read your sincerity. Recently, while driving with a group of youth, our conversation drifted toward church activities. One individual who was intimately involved with the youth readily picked up the fact that the leader really did not have their best interest at heart. How could they arrive at such a conclusion? Through simple observation.

The Bible refers to Jesus as a counselor. When you study the life of Christ, you come to realize that Christ was nothing more than a window into the personality of God—who and what God is. He is an intimate God with feelings and emotions, a personal God who literally became intimately involved with the issues of his clients. Condescension involves God becoming one with man. To understand the full impact of this, John, the writer of the fourth Gospel, states, "And the Word was made flesh, and dwelt among us, (and we beheld his glory, the glory as of the only begotten of the Father,) full of grace and truth" (John 1:14–15).

The Greek concept of deity established a core set of beliefs in the mind of a believer that gods never intimately involved themselves with the human. Their realms of living were always separate and far apart. John's burden in writing to Greek believers is to show the distinctive difference with his God. John shows an intimate God becoming one.

John establishes a God who does not dwell in a different sanctum but a God who is social—who sits, eats, socializes, and rubs shoulders with believers. As I have stated earlier, Christ was accused of being a glutton and a drunkard (Luke 7:33–34; Matt. 11:18–19), because He gathered often with people. There were times where the Bible records Jesus showing emotions such as at the graveside of Lazarus where "Jesus wept" (John 11:35). So John displays a type of God who is intimately involved, different from the normal Grecian god, who never socialized with their creatures. Provided, Christ is our example for counseling; we too must become involved with our youth or those whom we are counseling. Once the counselee begins to get a glimpse of who the counselor is, the opportunity for nouthetic confrontational counseling becomes less problematic.

Principles and Standards: Confusing?

When growing up as a church regular, I vividly remember hearing the words *principles* and *standards* used interchangeably. However, as a serious youth trying to get a grip on my religious experience, speakers did a very poor job distinguishing between the two. As a matter of fact, more often than not, I was left confused. For a very long time I actually thought they were one in the same. As the years passed and I became a thinking and studious youth, I learned to make the distinction myself. Discovering that there was a vast difference between the two made a tremendous difference in my approach to Christian living. Some youth never distinguished between the two, thus vacating church premises until they worked it out.

A definition of legalism is when there is a list of things you do to win the satisfaction of God in order to become a permanent resident in heaven. Once you accomplish this list of good deeds, you have obtained your spot. That, in essence, is what legalism is all about. However, legalism is what you want to avoid as a developing adolescent. The earlier you learn to distinguish between principles and standards, the better you will enjoy your Christian experience. My parents and adopted guardians through the church were, in essence, legalist—well meaning, but legalist. One thing I have discovered is more often than not, religionists tend to lean more toward legalism. When the Christian experience becomes legalistic, it is no longer fun.

One major area that can clear up confusion in Christianity for the adolescent is this distinction. In my personal research, questionnaires were disbursed to more than four hundred adolescents, subsequently revealing a lack of clarity. As the adolescent neared the college level of education, the understanding between the two became more defined through acquired knowledge. A quick way I discovered to distinguish principles from standards is that we never argue over principles; we just accept them. On the other hand, when it comes to standards, we tend to argue and engage in endless discussion and debate.

Principles are basically timeless truths defined by God in scripture, superseding time, space, and culture. Principles stir, supervise, guide, or pilot the Christian or believer's life, helping him to filter his choices by giving direction to the decision-making process. Principles are not considered big issues in Christianity; we just accept principles as truths given from God, considered basic doctrine or fundamental beliefs.

Where religious principle governs, the danger of committing great error is small. Principles of religious conviction governed the lives of many of our great men and women, which resulted in great change in society. To have firm religious principle is the purest, highest, and most elevated influence mortals can possess, because principles are derived and defined by God (see Diagram D: Principles and Standards). Stating it simply, principles are superior to standards.

Standards, on the other hand, are a set system of values and beliefs defined and created by individuals, institutions, and cultures. Standards are considered to be the application of principle. Standards may vary and change among individuals and institutions over time and space and varying between cultures. Standards are spawned from principles. A quick distinguishing conclusion is that principles are set by God, and standards are set by men.

Diagram D: Principles and Standards

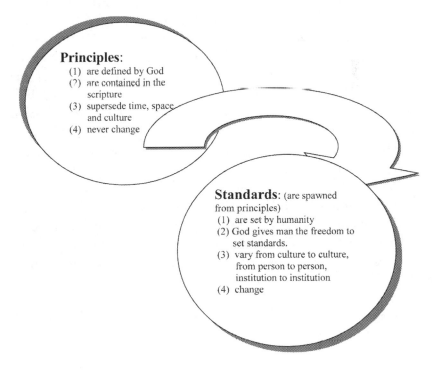

Principles:
(1) are defined by God
(?) are contained in the scripture
(3) supersede time, space and culture
(4) never change

Standards: (are spawned from principles)
(1) are set by humanity
(2) God gives man the freedom to set standards.
(3) vary from culture to culture, from person to person, institution to institution
(4) change

As stated earlier, oftentimes principles and standards are used interchangeably in Christian circles, making no distinction between the two and creating difficulty for the adolescent. Biblically, there are principles of dress—modesty and simplicity (Matt. 6:25–33), principles of moral value (John 2:16), principles of practicality and economy (1 Tim. 2:9), principles of health and diet (1 Cor. 3:16; Lev. 11; Deut. 14), principles of tithing (Mal. 3:8–10), principles of keeping the Sabbath (Ex. 20:8–11), and principles of worship (John 4:24). The principles of God were instituted with a broad base with set safety parameters, giving allowance for freedom and expression of the individual above and beyond set standards created by an individual, group, or institution.

This distinction must be clarified to adolescents, because standards often set by individuals, groups, or institutions become demanding rules or laws. Consequently, to the adolescent and believers the standard set by the individual, group, or institution (which now has become law) becomes misunderstood and confusing, creating an unhealthy environment for adolescent growth and development and sometimes creating a rebellious spirit. Because the adolescent sees human standards superseding biblical principles set by God, the message of Christ (the church) becomes skewed and confused with that of the messenger (humanity).

Many of the issues that Christian adolescents struggle with in the church are not, in essence, principles but are instead standards by church leaders. Gary Russel,[83] writing relative to standards, states that baby boomers are more interested in the principles behind the standards than in the standards themselves. Russell further states, "Baby boomers consider standards to be applications of principles and thus open to modification as time and culture require."[84] Greg Brothers, writing relative to standards, states, "standards are rules of thumb we've come up with over the years. Some we got from books; some we learned from others; some we had to figure out on our own. They are tools . . . they are good tools, important tools, tools we would be foolish to throw away needlessly but they are only tools. What is important is not the tools themselves, but the life you build on them."[85]

---

[83] Gary Russell, *"Boomers Call for a Socially Conscious Church,"* Adventist Today, (Nov./Dec. 1993) 88.

[84] Ibid.

[85] Gregg Brothers, *"Frogs, Toads, and Church Standards,"* Adventist Review (Jan./Feb. 2003), 23-25.

While Brothers may not agree to dismiss certain standards (because we tend to need them), he does agree that some of the standards Christianity cling to make denomination religion "peculiar" or "unique."[86] Another prominent authority figure, of whom I interviewed which prefers to remain anonymous states, "There are certain standards that the church cannot defend biblically . . . . We would rather say . . . some of the standards in question that we want to cling to—so to speak—is like the uniform of the church."

In essence, Genesis 1 presents a God who stresses variety, which is a trademark of His creative works. God does not robotically manipulate His children, expecting all to be the same. Instead, He encourages and allows diversity and creativity. When God sets the principle, He gives His children the liberty to exercise their differences or diversity within the parameters of the principle, allowing the individual to set the standard.

Principles give allowance to freedom. Keep in mind that standards are set from individual to individual, family to family, culture to culture. The standard will never be higher than or supersede the principle. Standards are the by-product of principle. We often refer to credible people by saying, "He sets a high standard for living."

Academic standards differ from institution to institution, but the principle for academic excellence is placed by a higher source within the academic arena. Consider Diagram E. I often give this little test to adolescents to help teach them to distinguish between what is considered a principle and what is considered a standard. Most times, they pick up the difference after having a few sessions.

When biblical principles are interpreted from scripture and taught properly, they give the adolescent freedom to think, greater respect for God, and improved parental communication. It also decreases the church dropout rate and lessens unhealthy interpersonal relationships between adolescents and authority figures.

Biblical teachers/instructors, spiritual guardians, and pastors must be careful that the message of God does not become confused with the messenger, creating unrealistic negative standards or expectations for the adolescent rather than positive, practical biblical principles set by God.

---

[86] Ibid.

Diagram E: Principles and Standards

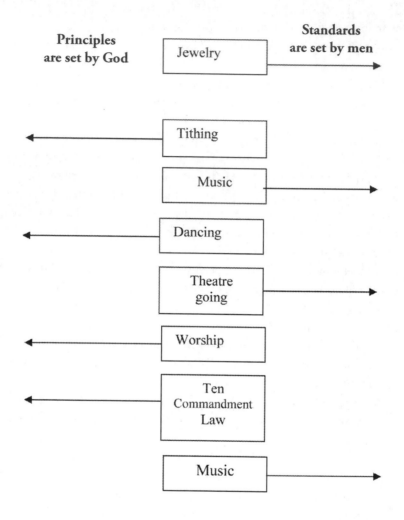

CHAPTER EIGHT

3-C COUNSELING MODEL

The 3-C counseling model approach is defined as the short-term approach to counseling facilitated by Christ Himself. This model involves three steps: 1) conference, 2) confronting, and 3) closure. This approach to counseling is quite easy to remember. When studying for my advanced degree, I learned what is called the Functional Dynamics of the Process Model (FDPM). The FDPM is a ten-step, linear process:

1) Building involvement
2) Gathering the data
3) Isolating the problem
4) Determining the direction
5) Rethinking the problem
6) Confronting the issue
7) Giving hope
8) Gaining a commitment
9) Assigning homework
10) Evaluating the homework

Frankly speaking, because I do not have the type memory where I can recall each of the ten steps in FDPM counseling model, I was forced to find a more contracted model unimpeded by my personal handicap of forgetfulness when engaging a counselee. Instead of remembering each step individually, I lumped several steps together, using all ten in a convoluted format. At the same time, I omitted some steps altogether. Yet, I still arrived at the same conclusion—data gathering.

While pastoring, the 3-C model has proven to be quite effective and very practical, because most pastoral or lay counseling is done on a short-term basis rather than long-term. However, while the 3-C model is designed for short-term counseling, it can also be used by licensed counselors, in each individual session, over an extended period. This approach as for long-term counseling—long-term in the sense that it can be used in each individual session should the counseling period become extended. If the counseling sessions should happen to become long-term in duration, the 3-C model becomes second nature in-that it becomes easier to follow, as an outline that fits both long- and short-term counseling. Let's consider each step individually.

Step One: Conferencing

There are really three components to conferencing: listening, talking, and gathering data. Adolescents really enjoy talking. As I often say of youth, they can get on a roll when talking and spill their guts. Even introverts will express themselves freely when there is a certain level of trust and security.

The problem comes in finding that adult with qualities of a confidante—individuals with high levels of trust and security. When dealing with adolescents, it needs to be remembered that as pastors, lay workers, counselors, and youth directors, you will have adolescents in the office of your lives quite often.

Change is constantly taking place in their lives. With my son, I am forced to keep my phone near me most of the time. While parents tend to hold on—and I do suggest letting go—move cautiously as you see that your child has begun to be more responsible in her decision making. Until then, keep your phone near. Good Christian counselors meet the criteria of confidante, because Christian graces are possessed.

Step Two: Confrontation

Confronting issues is never an easy task; however, as uncomfortable it may seem to be, it must be done. The story of ten-year-old Robert illustrates it best: Robert needed serious confrontation and ended up better for it. Robert was a wild and uncontrollable kid. When a dentist ordered Robert in the chair, Robert refused repeatedly, finally threatening to take his clothes off if the dentist made him get in the chair.

"Take 'em off," the dentist replied.

Robert took off everything but his pants.

"Okay, son, get into the chair," the dentist repeated.

"You don't understand—if you make me, I'll take all my clothes off!" Robert insisted.

"Son, take them off," the dentist ordered.

The boy complied and got into the chair, naked as the day he was born. When the dentist finished the procedures, Robert asked for his clothes back.

"I'm sorry, Robert, but we'll be keeping them for the night," the dentist said. "Your mother can pick them up tomorrow."

Can you imagine the shock in the waiting room when Robert made his nude exit? The mother returned the next day for the clothes and reported, "Robert has been blackmailing me with his clothes for years, but you're the first person to call his bluff. You have no idea what an impact this had on him."[87] Again, confronting others may be uncomfortable at times, but it must be done.

There are countless occasions biblically where Jesus confronted with truth (nouthetically) those with whom he came in contact. Keep in mind that we have already concluded that confronting involves three elements: the problem, the solution, and the motive by which the act has been committed.

Sin, is an act that comes from the heart. The goal of nouthetic counseling is to move the adolescent away from the sin that has been committed and to set forth plainly the will of God by bringing him into loving conformity to God's law. Counseling seeks to reverse the course of sin by awakening the conscience to righteousness and turning the adolescent toward God in repentance.

When dealing with Adam and Eve, God did not allow them to get away with what they had done. Adam tried with the act of blame shifting, attributing the act to Eve, and she did the same by passing it on to the serpent. The guilty one is the one who initially committed the act. This is confronting, or taking responsibility for your own actions.

---

[87]   James Dobson, *"Focus on the Family"*, April 2004.

Face-to-Face Confrontation: Confronting the issue is really not the problem. The problem comes when you must sit down and confront the individual(s) or when people have to confront each other. People do not enjoy being called out, especially when it is done before the one who was wronged. The time will come when there is a sit-down conference between parties where apologies need to be made. In order to keep parties from attacking the messenger or mediator, where tension is involved, it is always best to meet with individual parties in private, point out the discrepancies, and from a mediatorial perspective tell them your conclusions while alone. Then, bring parties back together so that no one will be caught by surprise. When that is done, the parties should correct wrongs before each other biblically.

Recorded in Luke 18:18–30 is a story where the nouthetic approach to counseling seemingly failed. It is the story of the rich young ruler, where Christ confronts the issues of the heart. However, when you review the story, you see that Jesus placed the decision at the center of the young man's heart.

The job of the counselor is to help point out the sin or the issues of the heart, while at the same time bringing truth. Immediately, Jesus puts his finger on the sore spot to point out the problem. The Bible says when this was done, the young man "went away sorrowful" (Matt. 19:22). Failure here resulted in the counselee not actually wanting to deal with the issues of his heart; thus, his sin remained. Keep in mind that the counselor's job is specifically to point out the issues of the heart and try to bring conformity to righteousness. Now that the issues, or sins, have been pointed out, where do we go? We bring closure.

Step Three: Closure

A definition of closure is simply to bring to an end. Closure is giving a sense of positive direction to the decision(s) made. Jesus never left anyone with whom He came in contact with hanging. Christ always brought closure as He encountered men and women in their sinful condition. The woman who was caught in adultery—after finding her in an entrapped situation, Christ forgave her of her sin and said simply, "Go, and sin no more" (John 8:11). To not bring closure is like leaving an open, gaping, festering wound. Draw conclusions by recommending positive change.

Oftentimes, counselors fail to bring closure. What's the sense of pointing out the wrong without recommending positive change?

There is law in nature that requires filling gaps and holes. This is also reality with the human experience. The question is asked: When does an alcoholic cease being an alcoholic? When he stops drinking? No, it's when he is "ceasing to do evil and start learning to do well." The Bible simply states, "overcome evil with good" (Rom. 12:21). Here is where victory lies for the child who is attempting to make the change.

Case Study: The Woman at the Well (John 4:1–42)

One of the titles given Jesus in scripture is counselor (Is. 9:6). As a matter of fact, Christ's method of counseling was short-term. Here is a situation where Jesus is at His best; He has a one-on-one encounter with a woman who has no hope of anything getting better. The Bible says she was a Samaritan, a people who were considered a Heinz 57 of Jesus's day—mixed heritage, not having "pure" blood. Instead, they were considered half-breeds, which made them an ostracized and rejected people living in the heart of Palestine.

Knowing the cultural dynamics that existed during this time, Jesus decided to take a more direct route to Jerusalem rather than the alternate route taken by the majority of the people in her day as a way to avoid contact with Samaritans. Jew and Samaritan were considered bitter enemies. They avoided any form of contact and dealing with each other except under dire emergency. To trade with the Samaritans in case of necessity was counted lawful by the rabbis, but all other social interaction was forbidden and condemned by the stated laws of the land. The groups didn't even exchange so much as a loaf of bread.

The disciples, in buying food from the Samaritans, were acting in harmony with the custom of their nation. But beyond this custom of purchasing food, they refused to go. To ask a favor of the Samaritans or in any way seek to help them did not enter into the thoughts of even Christ's disciples. Christ, in speaking with this woman, superseded the cultural mores of the day. To many Bible readers, the lady in the story has come to be known as just the "Woman at the well." I would suggest reading the story in its entirety.

The Human Need: Women in the orient were stigmatized and treated a little better than domesticated farm animals. It is very apparent that the lady had some issues. The Bible tells us she had been "married five times, and the man she was living with was not her husband" (John 4:18). She was shacking up with a live-in partner and carrying baggage from each relationship until she finally gave up on the institution of marriage and decided to just coexist with her male counterpart. You would think one or two failed relationships would be enough to devastate anyone, but five failed relationships, bordering on number six, would leave you without hope of things getting any better. Apparently, the institution that was designed to make life better was making life progressively worse for this anonymous lady. To sum her life up, it may well have been a case of her looking for love in all the wrong places until she finally gave up completely, and that's when she unsuspectingly met Jesus.

Christ, subjecting himself to humanity, found himself faint from hunger and thirst and seated at a Palestinian well, awaiting the service of one of His despondent children. Who comes? A Samaritan woman who had been separated by a racist society and had personal issues and needs that could only be filled by Christ, the supreme counselor. Unconscious of Christ's presence, the woman filled her pitcher and turned to leave. Suddenly, she was stopped by Jesus, who asked for a drink (a favor no Oriental in Jesus' day would withhold).

The Conference: Water was called "the gift of God," considering the climate, and to offer a drink to the thirsty traveler was held to be a duty so sacred that the Arabs of the desert would go out of their way in order to perform it. Hatred between Jew and Samaritan prevented the woman from offering kindness to Jesus, but Christ was seeking to find the key to her heart—a heart that had been broken and shattered by pseudo love experiences of the past.

Upon Christ's request, the woman realized that Jesus was a Jew and was taken by surprise. She actually forgot the initial request but tried to comprehend the reason for His questioning: "How *is it*," she said, "*that* thou, being a Jew, askest drink of me, which am a woman of Samaria?" (John 4:9). You can read the exclamation and consternation in her question.

Jesus answered and said to her, "Everyone who drinks of this water will thirst again; but whoever drinks of the water that I will give him will become in him a well of water springing up to eternal life." [NKJV] Because

Christ could read hearts and was very much aware of cultural dynamics of the times, He initiated the conference, breaking her preoccupation, which was temporal, physical water; Christ was concerned with that deeper need, spiritual water.

Not fully considering the one with whom she was speaking, she saw before her only a thirsty, way-worn, dusty traveler, no different in appearance than any other man she had encountered before. He only differed in race. However, she compared Christ to the Samaritans honored father Jacob, further engaging the conversation. "Sir, you have nothing to draw with, the well is deep, from where can you get this living water; are you as great as our father Jacob, which gave us the well and drank from it himself?" she asked.

While she was looking back to her father Jacob and the forefathers—the ones whom she respected and who looked forward to the One, the Messiah who was coming—she failed to realize that the One with whom she sat and spoke with was He. Christ was seeking something greater—to draw her attention away from herself, her issues, and to Himself and what he could give her. She was concerned with the temporal (physical water), while Christ was concerned with something higher (spiritual water).

As Jesus spoke of the living water, he finally broke from the norm of everyday conversation, arousing her interest, breaking her preoccupation, and awakening a desire for the gift of which He spoke that only He could give. She perceived that it was not the water of Jacob's well, her temporal spiritual father, to which He referred, because she used that water continually, drinking and thirsting again. "Sir," she said, "give me this water, that I thirst not, neither come hither to draw" (John 4:15).

The Confrontation: Jesus now abruptly turned the conversation. Before she could receive the gift that He wanted to bestow, she must be brought to recognize her sin and the need of a Savior. He said to her, "Go, call thy husband, and come hither" (John 4:16).

She answered, "I have no husband" (John 4:17). Her response was not misleading, but it was such that she did not want to reveal skeletons hidden in her closet or air the dirty laundry that stained her past and present life of which she was ashamed. So she sought to prevent all questionings in that direction.

However, the persistence of Jesus prevailed. "for you have had five husbands, and the one whom you now have is not your husband, this you have said truly." [NKJV]

Now what will she do? Christ had gotten into her private life (an area she wanted to avoid) and laid out her past, which she forever wanted to be hidden until the judgment. She did not want to make mention of the issues hidden in her heart, but Christ confronted her.

After Christ revealed the issues of the heart, the woman became evasive, hoping to silence conviction. Without denying anything, but with respect and reverence, she shifted to points of religious contention between Jew and Samaritan. She became concerned with the place of worship, while Christ was concerned with the essence of worship. She was concerned with the temporal, while He was concerned with the spiritual. Truly, we can understand this lady. Who wants to talk about six spoiled bedroom relationships back in her past? Patiently, Jesus permitted her to lead the conversation. Patiently, Jesus waited for the opportunity to bring truth home to her soul.

In answer to the woman, Jesus said, "Believe me, the hour cometh, when ye shall neither in this mountain, nor yet at Jerusalem, worship the Father. Ye worship ye know not what: we know what we worship: for salvation is of the Jews." Jesus had shown that He was free from Jewish prejudice against the Samaritans. Now He sought to break down the prejudice of this Samaritan against the Jews. While referring to the fact that the faith of the Samaritans was corrupted with idolatry, He declared that the great truths of redemption had been committed to the Jews and that the Messiah would appear from among the Jewish people.

In the Sacred Writings, the Jews had a clear presentation of the character of God and the principles of His government. Jesus classed Himself with the Jews as those to whom God had given a knowledge of Himself. Christ desired to lift the thoughts of His hearer above matters of form and ceremony and questions of controversy. "'But the hour cometh,' He said, 'and now is, when the true worshippers shall worship the Father in spirit and *in* truth: for the Father seeketh such to worship him. God *is* a Spirit: and they that worship him must worship *him* in spirit and *in* truth" (John 4:23–24).

There is more confrontation. In this story, the same truth is declared that Jesus had revealed to Nicodemus when He said, "Except a man be born again, he cannot see the kingdom of God" (John 3:3). Men are not brought into communion with heaven by seeking a holy mountain or a sacred temple. Religion is not to be confined to external forms and ceremonies, as the woman was concerned with the place of worship, but more so, the religion that comes from Christ is the only religion that will lead to God.

In order to serve God, we must be born of the divine Spirit, and only this will purify the heart and renew the mind, giving a new capacity for knowing and loving God. This woman needed a spiritual renewal, which is indeed true worship. It is the fruit of the working of the Holy Spirit. By the Spirit, every sincere prayer is indited, and such prayer is acceptable to God. Wherever an individual reaches out after God, the Spirit's working is obvious, and God will make Himself available to that individual. Such was the case with this woman. Christ wanted to make this woman a daughter of the kingdom.

As the woman conferred with Jesus, she was impressed with the Master's words. Never had she heard such sentiments from the religious leaders of her own people or from the Jews. As Jesus revealed the past of her life before her, she was made sensible of her great want. He had created a thirst in her soul that the waters of the well of Sychar would never satisfy. She'd had contact with men before, but no other man had so awakened her to a higher need. Jesus had convinced her that He read the secrets of her life, yet she felt that He was her friend, pitying and loving her, neither condemning nor ostracizing her.

It was the very purity of Christ's presence that condemned the sin in her life. He had spoken no word of denunciation but told her of His grace, renewing her soul. From this conversation, she began having some conviction of His character and who He was, prompting the question in her mind—could this be the long-looked-for Messiah?

She said to Him, "I know that Messiah cometh, which is called Christ: when He is come, He will tell us all things." Jesus answered, "I that speak unto thee am *he*" (John 4:26). As she heard these words, faith leaped in her heart, resulting in her acceptance of Christ as the long-sought-for Messiah. She became appreciative, ready to receive the noblest revelation, interested in the scriptures, and the Holy Spirit had been preparing her mind to receive more light. She had studied the Old Testament promise, "The Lord thy God will raise up unto thee a Prophet from the midst of thee, of thy brethren, like unto me; unto him ye shall hearken" (Deut. 18:15). Truth and light was already flashing into her mind. The water of life that only Christ could give to every thirsty soul had begun to awaken in her heart. The Spirit of the Lord was working with her. It is in this manner that Christ thirsts for recognition. He hungers for the sympathy and love of His lost children just like this woman, longing with inexpressible desire that they should come to Him and have life.

The Closure: The woman had been filled with joy as she listened to Christ's words. The revelation was so overpowering that she left her water pot and returned to the city, carrying the message to others. Jesus knew why she had gone. By leaving her water pot, she spoke unmistakably as to the effect of His words. It was the earnest desire of her soul to obtain the living water, and as a result, she forgot her errand to the well and also forgot the Savior's thirst.

With her heart overflowing with gladness, she hastened on her way to impart to others the revelation she had received. "Come, see a man, which told me all *things* that ever I did," she said to the men of the city. "Is not this the Christ?" (John 4:29).

Her words touched their hearts. I can imagine there was an expression on her face and a change in her entire appearance. She spoke with such strong sentiments that they were interested to see Jesus. The scripture tells us, "Then they went out of the city, and came unto him" (John 4:30).

In the words Christ spoke to the woman at the well, truth had fallen upon her heart, reaping a harvest of the woman and other Samaritans who turned to Christ. Crowding about Him at the well, they plied Him with questions and eagerly received His explanations of many things that had been obscure to them. As they listened, their perplexity began to clear away. They were like a people in great darkness tracing up a sudden ray of light till they had found the day.

But they were not satisfied with this short conference. They were anxious to hear more and to have their friends also listen to this wonderful teacher. They invited Him to their city, begging Him to remain with them. For two days Christ remained in Samaria, resulting in many more believers. Christ, with this lady, performed no miracle and showed no signs; he only revealed to the woman the secrets of her life. Jesus had begun to break down the partition wall between Jew and Gentile with this lady.

When Jesus sat down to rest at Jacob's well, He had come from Judea, where His ministry had little effect. He'd been rejected by the priests and rabbis, and people who professed to be His disciples had failed to perceive His character. He'd been faint and weary, yet He did not neglect the opportunity to give hope to a woman, a stranger and an alien from Israel. He revealed to her the "open sin" in her life, which resulted in her conversion. She found the Savior and drank of the living water, becoming a fountain of life, and the receiver became a giver. Christ, the ultimate short-term counselor, conferenced with her, confronted her, and brought closure to her life.

Common Sense Tips to Remember in Adolescent Counseling

Clearing the Air (Venting): When people talk, they are sometimes venting. Venting helps clear the air and provides opportunity for understanding. Another term for this biblically can be *confessing*. Recently, a beer summit was called by the president of the United States at the White House to help "clear the air" between himself, a university professor, and police officer regarding an incident where the two men had an altercation. Had the president not taken this measure, both public and private misunderstanding would have continued to prevail. Coming together helps bring solutions to issues. Many divorce settlements are solved relatively quickly when couples are forced by presiding judges to sit in private court backrooms along with their counselors to work out issues. The church actually provides the pulpit (forum) and the portfolio (method) for such discussion when adults sit and talk.

Two Sides to Every Story: Solomon was considered a wise counselor. There is a story of two women who bore children simultaneously. One woman's child died prematurely. The woman whose child died selfishly proceeded to kidnap the surviving child of the other, claiming the child to be hers. When word of the incident got to King Solomon, the king patiently listened to both sides before ordering that the child be severed in two. Of course, he knew that the real mother would step forward, not wanting to have her child dismantled with the sword and instead being willing to give up her child at any cost to spare the infant's life. A wise counselor listens to both sides before proceeding to make a final decision.

When certain issues are involved with adolescents, there is an old saying: no matter how thin the pancake, there are always two sides. Likewise, there are always two sides to every story. Here is another: there is my side, your side, and the right side. These statements tend to suggest that we study the arguments. Professional golfers who are good putters, Tiger Woods especially, tend to make good judgment calls, because they judge the path of the ball by studying the putting green from every angle. Study the arguments.

Furthermore, a testimony of two or three, according to the Bible, or more is always good; you began viewing the issues from every angle. When listening to adolescents and adults, try and help the other party view the issue from the other's perspective. Of course, studying the arguments may take some time. Never draw hasty conclusions.

Knowing When to Defer or Refer: Knowing when to quit is important. There are some issues of the heart that may be too deep for the lay counselor—for example, a case that may involve abuse where authorities need be brought in. This is a critical time when you do not cut them off, but instead defer or refer with Christian care. Always refer or defer to a certified Christian counselor. What you started can be finished in-depth with Christian psychological counseling, which can be very helpful in the society in which we live. Symptomatic behaviors deviating from the norm may also be a sign that it's time to refer or defer.

Fact Gathering: Gather the facts before you draw your conclusion. As a child I remember my father's favorite TV series *Dragnet*, where one Los Angeles detective, Joe Friday, became known for his favorite one-liner: "Only the facts, ma'am." Fact gathering is an attempt to arrive at truth with no intent of bringing harm or hurt to the counselee. In counseling you want as much as possible to focus on factual truths or data.

Conferencing is basically the data-gathering session where facts are obtained. There are times when data gathering takes time. However, here is the opportunity where good listening skills are facilitated. Fact gathering for Jesus came relatively easy. Christ could read hearts and minds of individuals. Because we cannot read hearts and minds, we must try our best to gather solid background data with objective listening skills.

You can start with the five Ws: who, what, when, where, and why. Lots of information can be sifted through interrogation. Many times, if the truth is not stated by the counselee (which can often be the case), eventually, the counselee will fumble over his words and leak contradictions. This sends up a red flag to question stated data. I often have a quote I state to members: "The truth will always surface. It may take some time, but the truth will always surface."

Stick to the Issue(s): I have been involved in discussions with colleagues where differences surfaced. The result was that those in authority veered from the issue(s) at hand and moved toward personal attacks and distractions with the tenor of the conversation becoming negative.

Attack the issue and not the person. It is always prudent to *stick with the issue(s)* and avoid the personal attacks and distractions. Moving into the personal creates a divide, further severing already-damaged relationships that may prove to be irreparable. Personal attacks create distrust, animosity, and resentment, distancing parties and individuals. Sometimes only time and the grace of God can heal these divisions.

Pray for Guidance: Keep in mind that the Holy Spirit is also a counselor. Prior to Jesus's departure from Earth, Christ said, John 14:16 "And I will pray the Father, and He shall give you another Comforter (Counselor) that He may abide with you forever." KJV. Angels are messengers of God whose outpost, or station, is planet Earth. These angels ascend back and forth from heaven, taking the prayers of men and women back to the very throne room of God. Angels are stationed beside us daily, listening to our prayers. It is my personal belief that genetically encoded in our tears are pains and hurts that only God can read transparently. When the lay counselor's heart is one with God, God will whisper in the ear of the counselor timely words in due season to speak at the right time to the counselee. I am suggesting to all that it's all right to cry; God reads your tears.

Keep Christ Central: Remember the goal in Christian counseling is to get the counselee to depend on Christ. All the counseling of Jesus was God-centered. Jesus was constantly pointing lost men and women to the Father. There will be times in the life of the adolescent when there will be no one near for them to talk to, but they must learn to reach out to Christ in prayer. The best prayers delivered to God by angels are from foxholes—pits of trouble. Daniel in the lions' den, Peter when sinking in the Galilean Sea, Paul in the Roman prison—all these men were alone and in trouble. When in deep trouble, we as humanity must learn to pray, keeping Christ at the center.

Personally, I have experienced comfort from heaven at the most inopportune times—behind the steering wheel of my car, in board meetings, during tests, etc. Hurts and emotions of the past have the tendency to slip into the backdoors of our lives, often catching us by surprise. Strangely, after communicating to God in prayerful release through my personal pain and tears, God gives a sense of consolation. The secular counselor would call this a moment of catharsis or release—getting it all out. From the Christian perspective, it is a time when God dispatches comforting angels, such as was in the case of Elijah. When he prayed for death, God sent an angel of life to comfort the flailing prophet in a time of desperate need and later sent him on his way. In the time of need, Christ will not forsake His hurting child but will help His weak child at any cost.

CHAPTER NINE

ELIHU: HE IS MY GOD

But Elihu son of Barakel the Buzite, of the family of Ram, became very angry with Job for justifying himself rather than God. (Job 32:2, NIV)

I want to close out with a different pitch, which sets the stage for this estranged, yet faithful adolescent, Elihu, of whom we hear little about. Let's make it crystal clear from the beginning that the first rebellious individuals were not developing adolescents but instead two intelligent adults with complete reasoning faculties. The biblical narrative unequivocally substantiates that sin came packaged in two responsible human beings with complete brain, muscle, fiber, and tissue.[88] As a matter of fact, they were literally established as replicas of Divinity, created in the very image of God. Every faculty of mind and soul of the created pair reflected God's glory.

Here were beings—balanced individuals, if you please—who had been endowed with the highest mental and spiritual capabilities, far above the rest of creation. They had been created "a little lower than angels" (Heb. 2:7) and were dwellers in Eden, the garden of God. They held face-to-face communion with God daily, and yet, with all this at their fingertips, they sinned. They erred in rejecting the authority of God, which is something that adolescents often receive blame for.

The fruit itself was definitely appealing to the eye and good to taste, because all that God had created in a sterile environment was good. But it was clearly stated: "God hath said, Ye shall not eat of it, neither shall ye touch it, lest ye die" (Gen. 3:3).

---

[88] Genesis 1:26–28.

"Do not touch!" was the stated command given by God. It was not the taste of the fruit that brought death but instead an act—an act of willful disobedience by two rebellious adults who rejected the voice of authority.

So the seed of rebellion was planted by two intelligent adults in a perfect state of human existence where angels hovered about them. Quite frankly, there was no excuse for their dreadful choice in a perfect environment. With their rebellious act, their posterity and the whole of creation became an endangered species, mentally, physically, spiritually, and socially.

Cain and Abel, the youthful posterity of Adam, would not have known the concept of sin had their parents not introduced to them this concept of brokenness. Irresponsibility was passed to Cain by way of his parents, and Cain, in turn, displayed the supreme act of irresponsibility and disobedience in great measure by killing his brother. What a humbling experience for the first family. As a result, scripture states, "The Lord was grieved that He had made man on the earth, and His heart was filled with pain" (Gen. 6:6, NIV).

With that said, in light of this ginormous mistake by our foreparents, little need be said about the mistakes of the adolescents. However, let's consider another godly persona: Job. I want to end with an adolescent whom God used to correct an outstanding servant. His name was Elihu, which translated means, "He is my God."

Little is actually known of him, and very little is said about him. Like a shooting star in its brief brilliance at night, he shows up on the scene and sits quietly for a short time. Then he speaks up, shuts up, and disappears from the scene of action. His timing is perfect, and he appears to be a young man God needed most at that critical hour. The incident with this young man—and I would go so far as to say adolescent—is mentioned late in the story of Job in chapter 32.

He opens his discourse with more modesty than is displayed by the other three antagonists as they attempt to confront Job. Elihu differs from the other antagonists in that his monologue discusses the providences of God, which he insists are full of wisdom and mercy. He states that the righteous have their share of prosperity in this life (no less than the wicked), that God is supreme, and that it becomes us to acknowledge and submit to that supremacy since "the Creator wisely rules the world of which he made." He draws instances of benignity from, for example, the constant wonders of creation and of the seasons. Job 3237 consists entirely of Elihu's speech to Job. He is never mentioned again after the end of this speech.

The speeches of Elihu—who is not mentioned in the beginning of the book of Job—contradict the opinions expressed by the "friendly accusers" in the central body of the text that it is impossible that the righteous should suffer. These men state that all pain is a punishment for some sin. Elihu states that suffering may be decreed for the righteous as a protection against greater sin, for moral betterment and warning, and to elicit greater trust and dependence on a merciful, compassionate God in the midst of adversity.

Some question the status of Elihu's interruption and teaching sermon because of his sudden appearance and disappearance from the text. He is not mentioned in Job 2:11 where Job's friends are introduced, and he's not mentioned at all in the epilogue, Job 42:7–10, in which God expresses anger at Job's friends. But Elihu's preface in Job 32 indicates that he has been listening intently to the conversation between Job and the other three men. He also admits his status as one who is not an elder (Job 32:6–7). As Elihu's monologue reveals, his anger against the three older men was so strong that he could not contain himself (Job 32:2–4).

In order to understand the incident with Elihu, we must get an understanding of what was going on with Job. In Job 1:1–3, we have these words:

> There was a man in the land of Uz, whose name *was* Job; and that man was perfect and upright, and one who feared God, and eschewed evil. And there were born unto him seven sons and three daughters. His substance also was seven thousand sheep, and three thousand camels, and five hundred yoke of oxen, and five hundred she asses, and a very great household; so that this man was the greatest of all the men of the east.

There are not too many men in scripture who God labels as great. However, this is what God says about Job: "This man was the greatest of all the men of the east—for his righteousness."[89] Never has God spoken more

---

[89]   Job 1:1–8.

eloquently except in the person of Jesus Christ. The setting of the book of Job is somewhere in the Arabian Desert culture, scholars agree, far away from Israel. My reason for stating this is because there were worshippers of God outside of Abraham and the Israelites, and Job was one of those worshippers. Nevertheless, Job emerged from a domestic background common to his age yet was not a part of the Israelites.

Job was a filthy rich landowner who was honored and loved by his countrymen and was loved and blessed by God for his righteousness. He stands out, a lone majestic important figure in history, because of his personal experience with God rather than because of his relationship to his time or to his contemporaries. According to Ellen White's commentary, Moses wrote the book of Genesis and also the book of Job, which would be read with the deepest interest by the people of God until the close of time.[90]

The name *Job* has an Aramaic derivation that means "to treat as an enemy" or "the assailed one." It is very obvious from reading the book of Job he was *assailed* by the adversary—Satan. Tradition holds, and it was generally believed by the Jews, that sin was punished in this life. Every affliction was regarded as the penalty of some wrongdoing, either of the sufferer himself or of his parents.

It is true that all suffering results from the transgression of God's law, but this truth had become perverted. Satan, the author of sin and all its results, had led men to look upon disease and death as proceeding from God as punishment arbitrarily inflicted on account of sin. Hence, one upon whom some great affliction or calamity had fallen had the additional burden of being regarded as a great sinner.[91] God had given a lesson designed to prevent this type of thinking. The history of Job had shown that suffering is inflicted by Satan and is overruled by God for purposes of mercy.

So we have this same theme with Job; all this was done for the praise, the honor, and the glory of God. Satan brings affliction, pain, and suffering, and God brings peace, joy, and goodness. So Job's name means "assailed by Satan," and in one hour, bless his righteous heart, Satan (the assailant) hurls a challenge at God, accusing God of pampering his child and showering him with blessing. The adversary comes challenging God

---

90   Ellen White, *"Signs of the Times,"* (February 19, 1880).
91   Ellen White, Desire of Ages, 471.

to "remove your protective hedge, and I will have him cursing you by the end of the day" (Job 1:10).

In one hour, God "permitted" Satan to afflict Job and hurl all of his maledictive hate against him, but He would not allow Satan to take his life. Why God allows certain things to happen to some and not to others, I do not know. What I do know is that *He* is God.

Each survivor in this tragic story comes to tell Job of all the devastation within the same hour—one after another, hit after hit—how Job lost his life's saving, his real estate, his posterity, and his inheritance. The saying goes, "when you have your health and strength, you have everything." And as if the loss of property, family, and income was not enough, Satan launched a final assault against Job as if coming back to finish what he started and took his health.

Here is Job, whose name means "assailed one." From birth, he was awarded the title "assailed one," such that Satan would be on his heels like a hound, ready to trample, kill, and destroy. It is my understanding from the reading that Satan waited till the right time, when Job had garnered and peaked in life, his wealth, and his family security—at a time when he could rest on his laurels, pull his Armani robe about him, walk out on his veranda, scale his plush property, and say like Nebuchadnezzar: "is this not the greatest estate, in the Land of Uz, that I have built." But he did not do that. The Bible says he was perfect, and upright, and eschewed evil (Job 1:1). He gave a faithful tithe, faithful offering, attended church regularly, gave to the poor, paid his property taxes, maintained his health, and was not considered an Israelite.

So we pick up the story in scripture: his three closest friends (Elephaz, Bildad, and Zophar) come to Job, and keeping with tradition, in essense stating in their own way Job has done something to warrant such disaster?

It was and is always the strategy of the Satan, the adversary man, to look upon disease and death as proceeding from God as punishment arbitrarily inflicted on account of sin. Hence, one upon whom some great affliction or calamity had fallen had the additional burden of being regarded as a great sinner. Why serve God if I am a born sinner who is prone to make mistakes? What do I gain from serving a God from fear? Satan, the adversary is living up to his name—the "accuser of the brethren."

Job, according to God, was great in righteousness; on the other hand, with Satan and tradition, Job was a great in sin.

It's as if his friends were saying to him, "You have done something, Job. You are harboring some transgression. ... There is some specific personal, hidden sin that you are not sharing with us. ... What is it? Come forth with it!"

For many wearying hours, Eliphaz, Bildad, and Zophar accused Job of all kinds of evil. And the one thing they set forth in their argument is the philosophy of suffering. Their philosophy reflected the faulty thinking of the times then and the times in which we live. They are promoting the idea that misfortune, bad luck, calamity, trouble, adversity, trial, disaster, tribulation, pain, and suffering come as a result of sin. Because of what you have done, you are now being punished for it. But, again, Job was righteous. These men, who were considered wise, were from the East. There is something about men of the East. Remember the wise men? Where were they from? The East! Men of the East had gained a type of reputation for possessing wisdom.

Maybe it was the place where men set in small educated circles, or "colleges," entertaining group discussions and sorting out answers to the deep problems of life.

The friends' speeches are somewhat profound, yet not in harmony with God's will. As a matter of fact, they are redundant, covering the same ground, emphasizing the same ideas, and employing the same expressions—you have done something, Job, and you need to repent. What is it? Again, Job and his friends were steeped in tradition that claimed that suffering was always punishment for specific sin or sins. However, Job was not aware of such sin, and now in his answering, he was faced with the predicament of finding an explanation for his misfortunate.

So Job, the Bible says, goes into his defense, entering into a theological dialogue with his friends to vindicate or defend his "challenged integrity," and all Job talks about is himself and his piety. He tells his friends about how righteous he is and how the punishment he is receiving from God does not fit the crime—if there even is one. His friends become so fed up with his defense that the Bible says the following:

> So these three men ceased to answer Job, because he *was* righteous in his own eyes. (Job 32:1)

> Then was kindled the wrath of Elihu the son of Barachel the Buzite, of the kindred of Ram: against Job was his

wrath kindled, because he justified himself rather than God. (Job 33:2)

Also against his three friends was his wrath kindled, because they had found no answer, and *yet* had condemned Job. (Job 33:3)

What is self-righteousness? I am told as a Christian, we are to "pile all the good works you can into this life." Job loved the Lord, and you can tell by his works. He was indeed a righteous guy. If a right-standing before God could be gained by works, Job is assured acceptance and salvation. But I am not saved by my works of righteousness. I am saved by the righteousness of Christ and his shed blood. Self-righteousness is an attempt to gain acceptance or favor from God by my own works of righteousness. The song entitled, "Nothing but the Blood of Jesus" says, "What can wash away my sin? Nothing but the blood of Jesus. What can make me whole again? Nothing but the blood of Jesus." I am justified, pronounced or made righteous by faith: because of Christ's life and death, looking from Heaven downward and not from earth up.

Job, on the other hand, felt that he could justify himself to God by looking from Earth upward. It is the righteousness of Christ that justifies me and not my own righteousness. I am counseled to "pile all the good works I can into this life," but my works of righteousness will not save me. I am saved only by the blood of Jesus! My *sincere* works are the evidence of my faith and love for Christ. My wife can tell whether my love for her is sincere, just as God can tell whether my works for Him are sincere. I am saved from heaven downward and not from Earth upward.

Further reading: Job 33:12 says, "Look, in this you are not righteous, I will answer you, for God is greater than man." NKJV. Keep in mind that Job is not the writer, Moses is the writer, and he is penning this under inspiration. And Moses writes, in Job 32:1, "So these three men ceased to answer Job, because he *was* Righteous in his own eyes."

I question you as a reader. Would you ever say you are self-righteous? Or would you be more prone to say, "I am not self-righteous, let alone would I write about it." We are more prone to write the good, especially when we know we have done no wrong. For some of us, the heavens will fall before we confess we have done no wrong, especially when we know we have not. Listen to Job as he defends his righteousness. He insists he has been faithful to God:

Moreover Job continued his parable, and said, *As* God liveth, *who* hath taken away my judgment; and the Almighty, *who* hath vexed my soul; All the while my breath *is* in me, and the spirit of God *is* in my nostrils; My lips shall not speak wickedness, nor my tongue utter deceit. God forbid that I should justify you: till I die I will not remove my integrity from me. My righteousness I hold fast, and will not let it go: my heart shall not reproach *me* so long as I live. (Job 27:1–6)

Also consider Job 29:14–25:

I put on righteousness, and it clothed me: my judgment *was* as a robe and a diadem. I was eyes to the blind, and feet *was* I to the lame. I *was* a father to the poor: and the cause *which* I knew not I searched out. And I brake the jaws of the wicked, and plucked the spoil out of his teeth. Then I said, I shall die in my nest, and I shall multiply *my* days as the sand. My root *was* spread out by the waters, and the dew lay all night upon my branch. My glory *was* fresh in me, and my bow was renewed in my hand. Unto me *men* gave ear, and waited, and kept silence at my counsel. After my words they spake not again; and my speech dropped upon them. And they waited for me as for the rain; and they opened their mouth wide *as* for the latter rain. *If* I laughed on them, they believed *it* not; and the light of my countenance they cast not down. I chose out their way, and sat chief, and dwelt as a king in the army, as *one that* comforteth the mourners.

In Job 31:1–40, Job insists:

I made a covenant with mine eyes; why then should I think upon a maid? For what portion of God *is there* from above? and *what* inheritance of the Almighty from on high? *Is* not destruction to the wicked? and a strange *punishment* to the workers of iniquity? Doth not he see my ways, and count all my steps? If I have walked with vanity, or *if* my foot hath hasted to deceit; Let me be weighed in an even balance, that God may know mine integrity. If my step hath turned out of the way, and mine heart walked after mine eyes, and *if any* blot hath cleaved to mine hands; *Then* let me sow, and let another eat; yea, let my offspring be rooted out. If mine heart have been deceived by a woman, or *if* I have laid wait at my neighbour's door; *Then* let my wife grind unto another, and let others bow down upon her. For this *is* an heinous crime; yea, it *is* an iniquity *to be punished by* the judges. For it *is* a fire *that* consumeth to destruction, and would root out all mine increase. If I did despise the cause of my manservant or of my maidservant, when they contended with me; What then shall I do when God riseth up? and when he visiteth, what shall I answer him? Did not he that made me in the womb make him? and did not one fashion us in the womb?

If I have withheld the poor from *their* desire, or have caused the eyes of the widow to fail; Or have eaten my morsel myself alone, and the fatherless hath not eaten thereof; (For from my youth he was brought up *with* me, as *with* a father, and I have guided her from my mother's womb;) If I have seen *any* perish for want of clothing, or *any* poor without covering; If his loins have not blessed me, and *if* he were *not* warmed with the fleece of my sheep; If I have lift up my hand against the fatherless, when I saw my help in the gate: *Then* let mine arm fall from *my* shoulder blade, and mine arm be broken from the bone. For destruction *from* God *was* a terror to me, and by reason of his highness I could not endure. If I have made gold my hope, or have said to the fine gold, *Thou art* my confidence; If I rejoiced because my wealth *was* great, and because mine hand had gotten much; If I beheld the sun when it shined, or the moon walking *in* brightness; And my heart hath been secretly enticed, or my mouth hath kissed my hand: This also *were* an iniquity *to be punished by* the judge: for I should have denied the God *that is* above. If I rejoiced at the destruction of him that hated me, or lift up myself when evil found him: (Neither have I suffered my mouth to sin by wishing a curse to his soul.) If the men of my tabernacle said not, Oh that we had of his flesh! we cannot be satisfied. The stranger did not lodge in the street: *but* I opened my doors to the traveller. If I covered my transgressions as Adam, by hiding mine iniquity in my bosom: Did I fear a great multitude, or did the contempt of families terrify me, that I kept silence, *and* went not out of the door? Oh that one would hear me! behold, my desire *is, that* the Almighty would answer me, and *that* mine adversary had written a book. Surely I would take it upon my shoulder, *and* bind it *as* a crown to me. I would declare unto him the number of my steps; as a prince would I go near unto him. If my land cry against me, or that the furrows likewise thereof complain; If I have eaten the fruits thereof without money, or have caused the owners thereof to lose their life: Let thistles grow instead of wheat, and cockle instead of barley. The words of Job are ended.

Job is indeed a righteous guy. Who would not want Job as an elder, a CEO, manager, overseer, boss, or pastor? His firm stand on principle and truth would get him in trouble from time to time, as it did with his friends. He was a trusted man—a man of integrity, a man of morality, a man of credibility, a man who was desirous of meeting demands and setting high moral standards of God. His heart was in the right place for service, he wanted and desired to do the right thing, he sought and wanted to please God.

But in his defense of himself, he was "righteous in his own eyes" or "self-righteous," and he sought to "justify himself, rather than God." According to Elihu—a young man who was filled with the Spirit—Job was wrong (Job 33:12).

Job says, "I have made a covenant with my eyes; I will not even think of sinning by looking on a young woman" (Job 31:1). The Clear Word Paraphase states "at a young woman with my eyes." He wants God to weigh his motives (Job 31:6). He is blameless in his relationship with women (Job 31:9–12). He goes on and on and on and on and on *justifying himself* before God and man!

God was right from the beginning with Satan. Job was a righteous guy, and his motives were pure. But Elihu, a young man, "a passerby," who sat, listened, and heard all the arguments—a young man of respect who waited for his elders to cease speaking before responding—contradicts Job. He is disturbed. Here, it was not the wisdom from the aged and learned friends of Job, but that of a Godly adolescent. There are times when wisdom comes from individuals or sources least expected. On this occasion wisdom came packaged in a young man.

Conclusion

Now that Elihu has spoken, read Job's response:

> Then Job answered the Lord, and said, Behold, I am vile; what shall I answer thee? I will lay *mine* hand upon my mouth. Once have I spoken; but I will not answer: yea, twice; but I will proceed no further. ... Then Job answered the Lord, and said, I know that thou canst do every *thing*, and *that* no thought can be withholden from thee. Who *is* he that hideth counsel without knowledge? therefore have I uttered that I understood not; *things* too wonderful for me, which I knew not. Hear, I beseech thee, and I will speak: I will demand of thee, and declare thou unto me. I have heard of thee by the hearing of the ear: but now mine eye seeth thee. Wherefore I abhor *myself*, and repent in dust and ashes. (Job 40:3–5; Job 42:1–6)

In closing, can an adolescent lead a Spirit-filled life? The Bible is replete with biblical examples such as Joseph, David, Shadrach, Meshach, Abed-Nego, Daniel, and a host of others, and more so, Jesus Christ himself. Like Elihu, whose name means "God is my God," no matter how toxic the age in which we live, God can be the God who leads.

The End

BIBLIOGRAPHY

Adams, Jay. *Competent to Counsel.* Zonervan Publishing House, Grand Rapid, MI. 1970.

Anderson, D. (1996, Feb.). *How Did We Lose a Generation of Youth?* 48-53.

Bacchiocchi, Samuele. Dance in the Bible. *College and University Dialogue* (Dec 1999): 40-45.

Bemmelen, Peter. The Bible: How is it unique? *College and University Dialogue* (Jan. 1995): 25-30.

Beeson. L. The Adventist Advantage. *Dialogue* (Nov. 1992): 38-44.

Benjamin, L. T., jr. (1981). Preface. In L. T. Benjamin, Jr. (Ed.), *G. Stanley Hall Lecture Series* (Vol. 1, pp. 1-6). Washington, DC: American Psychological Association.

Benker, J., J. Mcdermott, R. Rycek, S. Stuhr, and Swartz, M. Adolescence Egocentrism and Cognitive Functioning during Late Adolescence. *Adolescence* Vol. 33, Issue 132 (2002): 745+.

Blanco, Jack. *Clear Word Paraphrase,* Hagerstown, MD, Review and Herald Publishing Association, 2003.

Bodley, John. *Cultural Antropology,* 4th Edition, Columbus, OH. McGraw Hill Publishing Company, (March 2005)

Boyatt, E. Report Card on Adventist K-12 Education. Hagerstown, Maryland. *Adventist Review* (May 2004).

Brantley, P., and D. Fryson. Can Education Be Adventist and Excellent, Too? Hagerstown, Maryland. *Adventist Review* (April 2004).

Brega, A. G., and L. M. Coleman. Effects of religiosity and racial socialization on subjective stigmatization in African-American adolescents. *Journal of Adolescence* 22, 2 (1999): 223-242.

Brothers, G. Frogs and Toads, and Church Standards. *Adventist Review* (2003-1542): 33-37.

Brown, Colin (Editor). *Dictionary of New Testament Theology Volume III.* Grand Rapids, Michigan: Zondervan Publishing House, 1971.

Brown, N. Liberalism as a form of Legalism. *Adventist Review* (2003-1525): 33-34.

Campbell, K. *Those Ugly Emotions.* Ross-shire, Great Britain: Christian Focus Publications, 1996.

Canon, C. Striving. Grasping, Worrying, Overprotecting and Driving Young People to Destruction. *Adventist Today* (May/June 1995): 36-39.

Case, S. Valuegenesis: Is Anyone Listening? *Adventist Today* (Nov./Dec. 1993): 31-32.

Charry, Ellen T. Raising Christian Children in a Pagan Culture. *The Christian Century* Vol. 111, Issue: 5, The Christian Century Foundation (Feb. 1994): 166-170.

Colson, C. *Answers to your kid's questions.* Wheaton, Ill.: Tyndale House Publishers, Inc, 2000.

Dudley, Roger L. *Why teenagers reject religion and what to do about it.* Washington, DC: Review and Herald, 1978.

_____. *Passing on the Torch: How to Convey Religious Values to Young People.* Hagerstown, MD: Review and Herald Publishing Association, 1986.

_____. *Why Our Teenagers Leave the Church*. Hagerstown, MD: Review and Herald Publishing Association, 2000.

_____. *When Teenagers Cry, help! How to counsel effectively*. Washington, DC: Review and Herald, 1981.

Dudley, R., and J. Kangas. *The World of the Adventist Teenager*. Hagerstown, MD: Review and Herald Publishing Association, 1990.

Dudley, R., and V. Gillespie. *Value-Genesis: Faith in the Balance*. Riverside, CA: La Sierra University Press, 1992.

Dudley, R., and C. Hernandez. *Citizens of Two Worlds*. Hagerstown, Maryland: Review and Herald Publishing Assoc, 1992.

Dupertius, R. Young Adults Make Adventism Their Own. *Adventist Today* (March/April): 50-55.

Donahue, M. J., and P. L. Benson. Religion and the well being of adolescents. *Journal of Social Issues* 51, 2 (1995): 145-160.

Donelson, E. (1999). Psychology of religion and adolescents in the U.S. *Journal of Adolescence* 22, 2 (1999): 187-204.

Dryfoos, Joy. *Safe Passage: Making it Through Adolescence in a Risky Society*. New York, New York: Oxford University Press, 1998.

Erikson, E.H. (1968). Identity: Youth and Crisis. New York: Norton.

Focus on Adolescent Services 2000, Focusonadolescentservices.org

Francis, L. Parental Influence and Adolescent Religiosity: A Study of Church Attendance and Attitude Toward Christianity Among Adolescents 11 to 12 and 15 to 16 Years Old. *The International Journal for the Psychology of Religion* (1993): 241-253.

Geidd, Jay. *Interviews with Jay Geidd*. New York, New York: Oxford University Publishing Company, 2006.

Goldstein, C. The Problem of Knowledge. *Adventist Review* (2003-1513): 17-18.

Gillespie, V., M. Donahue, E. Boyatt, and B. Gane. *Valuegenesis: Ten Years Later.* Riverside, California: Hancock Center Publications, 2004.

Hammerly, H. Adventist Going to the Movies. *Adventist Today* (July/Aug. 1997): 25-28.

Hayden, Keaven. Lifestyles of the Remnant. *Adventist Review* (January 2001).

Hayes, B. *Measuring Customer Satisfaction: Development and Use of Questionnaires.* Milwaukee, Wisconsin: Quality Press, 1992.

Howard, Carol. Passage Through Puberty, *Psychology Today* Volume 19, 20 (Nov. 1985): 20.

Hudson, T. Current Concerns of a Conservative Adventist. *Adventist Review* (2002-1543): 2-24.

Hunker, Paula G. Teens Behaving Badly. *Insight on the News* Vol. 16, Issue 26 (July 2000): 26.

_____. Teen Years Bring Change—by the Minute. News World Communication Inc., 2 (August 17, 1999).

King James Virgin Bible

Jones-Haldeman, M. Adorning the Temple. *Spectrum* 20, 2 (Dec. 1989): 49-55.

Korangteng-Pipim, S. *Receiving the Word.* Berrien Springs, MI: Berean Books, 1996.

Land, G. Adventist in Plain Dress. *Spectrum* 205, 2 (Dec. 1989): 42-48.

Lee, Harold. Principled or Responsible Dissent. *Adventist Review* (Jan. 2002): 21-22.

Lewis, Sydney. *A Totally Alien Life-Form—Teenagers*, 17. New York, NY: The New Press, 1996.

Livermore, Beth. (Sept.-Oct. 1992). Build a Better Brain, *Psychology Today* Vol. 25 45-51.

Lovinger, S., L. Miller, and R. Lovinger. (1999). Some clinical applications of religious development in adolescence. *Journal of Adolescence,* 22 (2), 269-277.

Lutz, J. The Right Education, Hagerstown, Maryland. *Adventist Review* (April 2004).

Maxwell, C. Mervyn. *God Cares Voume II.* Boise, Idaho: Pacific Press Publishing Association, 1985.

Mclarty, J. Doctrine and Theology: What's the Difference *Adventist Today*, (March/April): 38-43.

Mead, Margaret. *Coming of Age in Samoa.* Cambridge, London: Harvard University Press.

Nembhard, J. A Critical Thinker? Or Merely Critical? *Adventist Review* (June 2002): 28-31.

Netteburg, K., and T. Wheeler. Every Child Should Be Church-schooled, *Adventist Review* (2002-1527): 35-37.

Newman, D. Is the Church Afraid of Candor? *Adventist Today* (Sept./Oct. 1993): 20-24.

New King James Version Bible

Olson, K. *"Why Teenagers Act the Way they Do."* Loveland, Colorado: Group Book Publishers, 1987.

Ozorak, E. Social and cognitive influences on the development of religious beliefs and commitment in adolescence. *Journal for the scientific study of religion* 28 (1989): 448-463.

Pruitt, David. "*Your Adolescent.*" New York, New York: Harper Collins Publishers, 1999.

Reid, E. Life in the Adventist Eggshell. *Adventist Today* (Nov./Dec. 1993): 31-31.

Rock, C. Editor, *Perspectives-Black Seventh-day Adventist and Concerns for youth.* Hagerstown, MD: Review and Herald Publishing Assoc., 1996.

Rodriguez, Angel M. *Jewelry in the Bible.* Silver Spring, Maryland: Pacific Press Publishing Association, 1999.

Rogers, D. *The Psychology of Adolescence.* 2nd ed., New York: Appleton Century Crofts, 1972.

Russell, G. Boomers Call for a Socially Conscious Church. *Adventist Today* (Nov./Dec. 1993): 25-27.

Sandberg, K. Reid, C. Beating Up on Upbeat Music. *Adventist Today* (Sept./Oct. 2001): 25-31.

Sahlin, Monte. *Adventist Congregations Today.* Lincoln, NE: Center for Creative Ministry, 2003.

Scriven, C. "I didn't Recognize You With Your Ring On" *Spectrum* 20, 2 (Dec. 1989): 56-59.

Schiamberg, L. *Adolescent Alienation.* Columbus, Ohio: Charles E. Merrill Press, 1973.

Schafer, W. E., and M. King. Religiousness and stress among college students. *Journal of College Student Development* 31 (1990): 336-341.

Seventh-day Adventist Bible Commnetary vol 4. Washington D.C. Review and Herald Publishing Association. 1976

Seventh-day Adventist. 58th General Conference World Session, St. Louis, Missouri. USA, July 3, 2005.

Seel, John D. *Parenting Without Perfection.* Colorado Springs, CO: Navpress Publishing House, 2000.

Staples, R. Adventist in the 21st Century. (1995, May). *Adventist Ministry to College and University Students* (AMiCUS), 20-24.

Stewart, C. *Adolescent Religion.* Nashville, Tenn: Abingdon Press, 1967.

Tageson, C. *Spiritual Directions of the Adolescent in Psychological Counseling of Adolescents,* ed. Raymond Steimel. Washington, DC: Catholic University of America Press, 1962.

Taylor, E. Progressive Adventism. *Adventist Today* (Sept./Oct. 2001): 25-26.

Tripp, Paul. *Age of Opportunity.* Phillipsburg, NJ: P & R Publishing, 2001.

Tsubata, Kate. "Guidance in Rough Teen Years." *Washington Times*, March 22, 2004.

The Seventh-day Adventist Church Manual. Hagerstown, MD: Review and Herald Publishing Association, 1981.

The Seventh-day Adventist Church Manual. 16th Ed. Hagerstown, MD: Review and Herald Publishing Association, 2000.

Vance, D. Young Adults Probe for Meaning in an Uncertain World. *Adventist Today* (Nov./Dec. 1993): 40-45.

Wetzstein, Cheryl. "Why Children Need Limits." *Insight on the News* Vol. 12, Issue 41 (Nov. 1996): 41.

White, Ellen G. *A Call to Stand Apart: Selections from the writings of Ellen G. White.* Hagerstown, MD: Review and Herald Publishing Association, 2002.

_____. *Acts of the Apostles.* Mountain View, CA: Pacific Press Publishing Assoc., 1948.

_____. *Child Guidance.* Nashville, Tenn: Southern Publishing Association, 1954.

_____. *Desire of Ages.* Mountain View, CA: Pacific Press Publishing Assoc., 1948.

_____. *Education.* Mountain View, CA: Pacific Press Publishing Assoc., 1903.

_____. *Fundamentals of Christian Education.* Hagerston, MD: Review and Herald Publishing Association, 1923.

_____. *Message to Young People.* Mountain View, CA: Pacific Press Publishing Assoc., 1948.

_____. *Patriarchs and Prophets.* Mountain View, CA: Pacific Press, 1958.

_____. *Signs of the Times.* February 19, 1880.

_____. *The Adventist Home.* Nashville, Tenn: Southern Publishing Association, 1952.

_____. *Testimonies for the Church Vol 1*: Mountain View, CA: Pacific Press Publishing Assoc., 1948.

_____. *Testimonies for the Church, Vol. 3*: Appeal to the Young, Mountain View Pacific Press Publishing Assoc., 1948.

_____. *Testimonies for the Church, Vol. 4*: Mountain View, California. Pacific Press Publishing Assoc., 1948.

_____. *Testimonies for the Church Vol 5*: Mountain View, CA: Pacific Press Publishing Assoc., 1948.

_____. *Testimonies for the Church Vol 6*: Mountain View, CA: Pacific Press Publishing Assoc., 1948.

_____. Story of Redemption, Mountain View, CA: Pacific Press Publishing Assoc., 1948.

Yust, Karen Marie (Editor), Aostre N. Johnson (Editor), Sandy Eisenberg Sasso (Editor), Eugene C. Roehlkepartain (Editor), Ellen T. Charry (Contributor). *Nurturing Child and Adolescent Spirituality: Perspectives from the World's Religious Traditions.* Zondervan Publishing Company, Grand Rapids, Michigan. 2005

Unpublished Sources:

Banta, Harold E. *A study of why Seventh-day Adventist who attend Seventh-Day Adventist Schools separate from their church.* MA thesis, Loma Linda University, 1980.

Dudley, Roger L. *Selected variables related to alienation from religious as perceived by students attending Seventh-day Adventist Academies in the United States and Canada.* Ed. Dissertation, Andrews University, 1977.

Kanjas, Janet L. *A study of the religious attitudes and behaviors of Seventh-day Adventist adolescents in North America related to their family, educational, and church backgrounds.* Ed. Dissertation, Andrews University, 1988.

Laurent, Robert. *Selected variables related to alienation from religion among church-related high school students.* PhD Dissertation, Andrews University, 1986.